(Opposite page) All that remained of the buildings at the Scales, on the Alaska side of the Chilkoot Trail, in June, 1976.

(Right) Dyea Flats during the height of the Klondike stampede. Before the gold rush began, Healy and Wilson's trading post, not shown in this photograph, had been the only white residence in the Indian village.

(Below) The remains of the piers from the Dyea wharf. These, and a few scattered piles of lumber, are the only evidence left of the gold rush stampede through Dyea Flats, Alaska. (Below, inset) Chilkoot Jack," pictured here in ceremonial dress, guided the first white man to the Yukon. This photo was taken in 1899.

2, 1864: "There is a small river not far from here that the minister the Rev. McDonald saw so much gold on a year or two ago that he could have gathered it with a spoon. I have often wished to go, but could not find the time." When McDonald sent samples of coarse nuggets back to England, the London *Times* published an account of his discovery, but the HBC employees were too busy to prospect, and, once again, no one else paid any attention.

Emperor Nicholas of Russia, meanwhile, had offered to sell Alaska to the United States (U.S.) "for a nominal consideration" as far back as 1844. The Russians had only one condition, "that England should be shut out from any frontage on the Pacific Ocean." The offer, not then accepted, was several times renewed, and finally, in 1867, the U.S. purchased Alaska at the cost of $7,200,000, or about half a cent an acre.

Six years later, in 1873, the first independent prospectors began to dribble into the Yukon. The first of these was Arthur Harper. Born in the county of Antrim, Ireland, in 1835, he left it while yet a boy to try his luck in America. After spending some time on the eastern seaboard of the U.S., Harper gravitated towards the goldfields of the west, and by the late 1860s was in British Columbia (B.C.). Fortune eluded him, however, and he looked about for new, as yet untried, goldfields. After studying a copy of Arrowsmith's map of British North America, he concluded that an extensive goldfield lay undetected in the north. Harper convinced four others, Frederick Harte, a fellow countryman, George Finch, a Canadian, Andrew Kansellar, a German and Samuel Wilkinson, an Englishman, to accompany him. In September, 1872, having equipped themselves for a long journey and a protracted stay in the wilderness, the five men started out from Manson Creek in northern B.C.

Meanwhile, another group consisting of LeRoy Napoleon "Jack" McQuesten, Alfred H. Mayo and James McKnipp, all former employees of the HBC, were also planning to venture to the Yukon. The three had been wintering on the Hay River in the North West Territories in 1871 when tales related to them by HBC employees piqued their interest. By the fall of 1872 they had reached Francis Lake where they erected a cabin for the winter. In early November they were joined by three HBC employees who erected a cabin near them.

One evening Sibistone, one of the HBC employees, related an incident that had occurred at Fort Yukon while he was stationed there in 1869. Fort Yukon, constructed by Alexander Murray of the HBC in 1847, was more than 100 miles in Russian territory. Despite this, it conducted a prosperous and unmolested trade with the Indians for 22 years. The day of reckoning finally came in August, 1869, when the little steamer *Yukon,* carrying Capt. Charles Raymond of the U.S. Army, paid a visit. Raymond advised the HBC that they were trading illegally in what was now U.S. territory, and they would have to vacate the post as soon as practicable.

According to Sibistone, the Americans discovered gold near the fort: "Mr. Sibistone told us that one of the officers that came up on the steamer washed a jar of dirt near Fort Yukon and he had about a teaspoonful of something yellow in the pan and the officer threw it away remarking that it would not do to let the men see it as they would all leave the steamer." This information, later corroborated by Chief Factor McDougal, excited McQuesten, Mayo and McKnipp.

In the spring of 1873 the McQuesten party was joined by the five-man prospecting party headed by Harper. After some consultation, Wilkinson decided he had a better chance of finding gold on the Liard River and left on his own for that waterway. The others all agreed to go on to Fort Yukon, albeit by different routes. Accordingly, when the McQuesten party finally arrived at the Fort Yukon on August 21, Harper and company were already there, having arrived on July 15. They were all greeted by Moses Mercier, an agent for the Alaska Commercial Company (A.C.C.), who extended them every consideration and assistance. "We were treated like kings," wrote McQuesten. "We remained two days. Some of us had not such good living in ten years."

While at Fort Yukon, Harper met an Indian who had quite a chunk of native copper he said came from White River, more than 400 miles up the Yukon. Intrigued by the specimen, Harper, Harte and Finch decided to go to White River to investigate. Kansellar, however, choose to accompany McQuesten and the others down river. Along the way the Harper party panned the mouth of what would later be called Fortymile River. Here they found such good prospects that they were about to ascend the river to test it further. Had they done so, the gold rush to the Yukon Valley might have started 15 years earlier than it did. Unfortunately, fate, in the form of Indians

(Left) A typical Russian fort in Alaska before it was purchased by the U.S. government.
(Left) Robert Campbell, founder of Fort Selkirk.

FRONT COVER:
Interior of what was probably a roadhouse for travellers at Yukon Crossing in 1988.

PHOTO CREDITS:
National Parks, Canada: 2, 2-3, 59 (bottom left & right) and 85 (bottom right).
B.C. Provincial Archives: 3 (top), 4, 17 (top left), 26 (top), 42 (bottom), 47 (top left & top right), 48 (top & centre right), 56 (centre), 59 (top left) and 60 (top).
Yukon Archives: 3 (inset), 12, 17 (top right & bottom), 18-19, 19, 21, 26 (bottom), 30 (top), 41 (inset), 42 (top), 47 (bottom), 53, 60 (bottom), 73, 76, 77 (top), 86, 89 (top), 90, 91, 94 & 95.
Sunfire Archives: 5, 10 (inset), 18 (top left & right), 20, 22- 23, 29, 70 (bottom) & 71 (bottom).
Garnet Basque: 6 (top), 6-7, 14, 15, 33, 36, 37 (top), 44 (top left), 55 (top), 74, 75, 78 (top), 81 (top), 84, 85 (top left & bottom left), 88 (centre & bottom) & 89 (bottom).
Hudson's Bay Company: 6 (bottom).
John Stevenson: 7 (top).
National Archives of Canada: 7 (inset), 13, 30 (bottom), 38-39, 77 (bottom) & 88 (top).
Yukon Government: 10-11.
University of Alaska: 24.
Vancouver City Archives: 32, 34, 35, 37 (bottom) & 38 (top).
Barbara Kalen: 40-41, 44 (top right & bottom), 45, 48 (centre left & bottom), 50-51, 51 (bottom), 54 (top), 58 (centre), 62 (bottom) and 70-71.
Montana Historical Society: 40 (inset).
White Pass & Yukon Railway: 50, 56 (bottom), 63, 65, 66 (top), 67 & 68.
Roy Minter: 54-55 & 66 (bottom).
Minnesota Historical Society: 56 (top).
Jeffrey Murray: 58 (top & bottom).
Rand Snure: 62 (top).
M.J. Heney: 64 (left).
Seattle *Times*: 64 (centre).
Robert Wood: 64 (right).
Steve Hites: 66 (centre left & bottom left).
Stewart Breithaupt: 78 (bottom).
Roland Barnett: 79 & 85 (top right & centre).
George Tumpach: 81 (bottom).

FRONTIER DAYS IN THE YUKON

SUNFIRE PUBLICATIONS LIMITED
P.O. BOX 3399,
LANGLEY, B.C. V3A 4R7

PRINTING HISTORY
First Printing — August 1991

PRODUCTION CREDITS
Design, layout and maps — Garnet Basque
Typesetting — Kirkrod Printing, Vancouver
Printing — Colorcraft Ltd., Hong Kong

Canadian Cataloguing in Publication Data

Main entry under title:
Frontier Days in the Yukon

Includes index.
ISBN 0-919531-32-6

1. Yukon Territory — History — 1895-1918.*
2. Yukon Territory — History. 3. Yukon Territory — Biography. 4. Frontier and pioneer life — Yukon Territory. 5. Klondike River Valley (Yukon) — Gold discoveries. I. Basque, Garnet.
FC4022.F76 1991   971.9'102   C91-091460-5
F1093.F76 1991

PRELUDE TO BONANZA

For all intents and purposes, the arrival of two ships, the *Excelsior* at San Francisco on July 14, 1897, and the *Portland* at Seattle one day later, signalled the start of the Klondike gold rush. But this was not the first time gold was discovered in the Yukon, now was it the first gold rush to take place there.

THE Russians were the first to venture into what is now Alaska, their territory being ruled by Alexander Baranoff from Sitka. Like the Hudson's Bay Company (HBC), who would come later, the Russians were chiefly interested in furs. Both realized that the discovery of gold would precipitate a flood of miners into the region, and this would destroy the lucrative fur trade. When one of Baranoff's hunters showed him a handful of gold nuggets in 1804, his reaction is therefore not surprising. Warning that if word of the discovery reached the Americans or Englishmen, they would ". . .rush in on us by the thousands, and crowd us to the wall — to the death," Baranoff forbid the man to utter another word about his discovery. So for the next four decades, while they harvested rich fur pelts, the Russians suppressed the news.

Next to venture into the Yukon was the HBC. In 1840, under the command of Robert Campbell, one of their most industrious employees, a party of four whites and three Indian guides began to explore the Liard River. In July Campbell discovered and named Francis Lake, upon whose banks a post was constructed in 1842. When Fort Francis was successfully established, Campbell began to explore the Pelly River, which he had first explored in 1840, in greater detail. In 1848, following Sir George Simpson's latest instructions, Campbell ordered the construction of Fort Selkirk at the junction of the Yukon and Pelly rivers. Later the same year Campbell found traces of gold around the new fort, but the HBC, interested only in furs, ignored the find.

The next discovery was made in 1863 when Rev. Robert MacDonald, another HBC employee, found gold on Birch Creek in Alaska. One of the HBC clerks stationed at Fort Yukon described the find in a letter he wrote to his family on October

camped nearby, intervened. The Indians convinced Harper that there was an impassable canyon upstream that would surely claim all their lives if they attempted to pass. The Harper party, not realizing that the Indians were grossly exaggerating, decided not to risk the perceived dangers and instead continued on to White River.

McQuesten and his associates, meanwhile, had also been attracted to the Yukon by prospects of gold. However, upon hearing of the region's potential as a source of furs, they decided to try trapping for a year and went down river about 50 miles where they wintered. This proved unsuccessful, however, and in the spring of 1874 they abandoned their cabin at Rampart Canyon and returned to Fort Yukon where they waited for the ice to break up. On May 20 the Harper party joined them from upriver, and on June 4, Moses Mercier loaded both parties aboard his barge and started for St. Michael, arriving there 16 days later.

Francois Mercier, Moses' brother, who was in charge of the A.C.C. at St. Michael, offered all of them positions with the company. Mayo accepted and left to operate the post at Nukluroyit. Harte also accepted, but Harper, Finch and Kansellar declined. However, since they wanted to investigate a reported discovery of gold on a mountain near Nukluroyit, they decided to accompany Mayo to that post.

McQuesten also accepted the offer, and, with an assistant, proceeded upstream aboard the *Yukon*. On August 20, 1874, McQuesten selected a site not far from the Tron Deg (now Klondike) River and erected a post he named Fort Reliance. The Indians turned out to be such excellent customers that the three tons of trade goods were depleted by spring, and McQuesten headed down river to St. Michael to replenish his supplies. At Nukluroyit, McQuesten picked up a very disheartened Harper. His companions Finch and Kansellar had had enough and were quitting the north, but Harper, now broke and frustrated, agreed to accept a new offer from the A.C.C. He, McQuesten and Mayo were all to become free agents, an arrangement which would allow them each ample time to prospect.

During the next three years, at every opportunity, Harper picked and panned his way about the country. In 1875 he made a discovery on Sixtymile River that looked so promising he was determined to return the following year and sent out for a tank of quicksilver. Unfortunately, before it arrived, In-

dian trouble forced Harper to leave the area. By the time the Indian situation was resolved, Harper could no longer afford to give up his employment with the A.C.C. Once again fate had intervened for "Bad Luck" Harper. McQuesten, who examined the site of Harper's discovery in the fall of 1877, wrote: "I found Gold on all the bars in small quantities — I found some places where a man could make $6.00 to $8.00 per day but not extensive pay enough to put on a string of sluices."

Although Harper's employment with the A.C.C. did not allow him the opportunity to mine exclusively, he was becoming aware of the great potential of the Yukon, and his letters to friends on the outside helped to arouse curiosity and create interest. Those letters, and the Alaska purchase of a decade earlier, were beginning to attract a few adventuresome Americans, and gradually they began to sprinkle into the region. The first of these to prospect in earnest was George Holt, an employee of the A.C.C. In 1875, Holt became the first white man to enter the Yukon through the Chilkoot Pass, though how he managed to get past the Indians guarding the entrance remains a mystery. In 1880 Holt sent two small gold nuggets, the first to reach the outside world, to St. Michael. He claimed the gold had been given to him by a Tanana River Indian, but just where the Indian had found the gold is not known.

Although Holt never went back to the interior, the news he furnished enticed Edward Bean to lead a 25-man party into the region the same year. Protected by a U.S. gunboat, they debarked at Dyea Inlet, scaled the Chilkoot Pass and went down the chain of lakes which lead to the Yukon River. Although they found bars yielding $2.50 a day on a small tributary of the Yukon, it was not sufficient quantities to encourage them in further effort.

In 1880, lode gold was discovered at Juneau, Alaska. This discovery attracted drifters, frontiersmen and adventurers from all over the American west, and, inadvertently, led to the discovery of the rich Yukon goldfields. Gradually, in twos and threes, they drifted over the Chilkoot Pass and into the Yukon Valley.

"The fall of 1882," wrote McQuesten, "was noted for the number of men that came into the country to prospect for gold." The first party to come over the Chilkoot Pass that year included Joseph Ladue, who would later become the founder of Dawson City, John Rogers and John Frasier. They arrived

Three of the earliest white men to venture into the Yukon Valley: left, Arthur Harper; centre, Fred Harte and right, Jack McQuesten.

on September 5 with enough flour and provisions for two years. McQuesten took them over to Sixtymile River where they found "...very encouraging prospects about 15 miles below Miller Creek. Jo Ladue panned out several pieces that weighed .10 ct. The ground was frozen and we had to thaw out the ground by fires. It took us three days to sink one hole ten feet deep and the water came in so we had to abandon it before we got to bed rock. We got short of provisions and it was getting very cold so we returned home, and the party was well satisfied and intended to go back in the Spring. Shortly after we returned home seven more men arrived. They all built cabins and went into winter quarters. They were not so well supplied with provisions as the first parties. I had plenty of flour on hand and they all passed the winter and had plenty for the following summer."

In the summer of 1883 four men, Richard Poplin, Charles McKonkey, Benjamin Beach, and C. Marks, went over the Chilkoot Pass and down the Yukon, prospecting as they went, and when they reached the Stewart they ascended it to the McQuesten. They found gold on almost all the creeks they tried, and had recovered $10 a day with a rocker. By this time their supplies were running out, so they headed for Fort Reliance. Upon reaching the post they learned that the steamer had broken down on the lower river, and they had to continue to Tanana, where they wintered.

In the spring of 1884 McQuesten took them up the Stewart River on the *Yukon,* where they spent the summer prospecting.

(Opposite page, top) Grave of Fred Harte in the Yukon Order of Pioneers cemetery, Dawson. It reads: "Frederick Washington Harte, died Nov. 9, 1897. Aged 59 years. One of the earliest pioneers of the Yukon Valley 1873."

(Opposite page, bottom) This 1949 HBC calender depicts the building of Fort Yukon. This post had to be abandoned by the HBC in 1869 when it was found to be in American territory.

(Right) The Yukon River Valley, looking south from Dawson.

(Below) The foundations of the HBC's store at Fort Selkirk in the Yukon. Campbell established a post here in 1848. In 1852 it was raided by angry Chilkat Indians who pilfered the supplies and burned the post to the ground. When gold seekers passed through the region during the early years of the Klondike gold rush, only the two stone chimneys seen in the inset remained. The gold rush renewed interest in the area and Fort Selkirk was rebuilt. These foundations are from the gold rush era. Today, Fort Selkirk is undergoing an extensive restoration program.

In the fall they all went out over the Chilkoot Pass. On their way up the Yukon River they met Thomas Boswell and some miners who were working the banks and bars of the upper river. Poplin told Boswell that he could find plenty of better diggings on the Stewart River. Boswell and party took the hint, and went down to Fort Reliance where they remained through the winter.

In April, 1885, the Boswell group sleighed up the Stewart, prospecting the river as they went. This was done by building fires on the bars, thawing the gravel and washing it. They then marked any promising bars that were located, planning to return later. However, when they discovered Chapman's Bar, about 90 miles up, they found it so good that they determined to work it for the summer. The average per man for the season was about $100 per day, which, with rockers, was considered extraordinary.

Richard Poplin returned the same spring from Juneau with Peter Wybourg, Francis Morphat, and Jeremiah Bertrand, and went up the Stewart, passing the Boswell party at Chapman's Bar. About seven miles farther up they discovered what later came to be known as Steamboat Bar. Settling in for the season, they cleaned-up about $35,000.

Up to this time McQuesten had been carrying on a trade chiefly with the Indians, and, accordingly, had not stocked provisions necessary for miners, such as clothing, boots and tools. But, with the steady influx of men coming into the territory each year, he decided it was time to bring in these necessities.

Although McQuesten did not actively seek gold, as did Harper, he was nevertheless a strong supporter of mining activities. His efforts, as a trader, contributed greatly to the opening up of the Yukon Valley. Many old-timers frequently acknowledged McQuesten's "goodness of heart and leniency in collecting accounts." This can best be illustrated by an incident that occurred when a miner came in to pay his bill. Surprised at the amount he owed, the miner replied:

"Seven hundred! H--l, Jack, I've only got five hundred, how'm I goin' to pay seven hundred with five?

"Oh, that's all right, give us your five hundred, and we'll credit you and let the rest stand till next clean-up.

"But, Jack, I want some more stuff. How'm I goin' to get that?

"Why, we'll let you have it as we did before.

"But, d--n it, Jack, I haven't had a spree yet.

"Well, go and have your little spree, come back with what is left, and we'll credit you with it and go on as before."

Unfortunately, after the spree, there was nothing left, but McQuesten allowed him to charge another $500 bringing his total bill to $1,200, to be paid, hopefully, at the next clean-up.

On August 10, 1885, McQuesten landed at Fort Reliance with 50 tons of miners supplies. Aboard the little steamer was Joseph Ladue, Howard Franklin, Thomas Williams, Harry Madison and Mike Hess. They had all been prospecting along the Yukon River. When they landed at the post, Boswell was already there.

The Boswell and Poplin parties had made the most significant discovery in the Yukon to date, but Boswell, in betrayal of the unwritten miner's code, uttered not a word to the men at Fort Reliance. Instead, he informed the group that they had not found anything and were planning to trap for the winter.

Since McQuesten was going to Fort Selkirk to trade furs, he took the group of prospectors with him. When they reached Stewart River, Boswell went ashore. Franklin and Madison got off at White River where they prospected all winter with little success. Williams, Ladue and Hess went on to Selkirk where they built a boat and went on up the river to some bars that had been worked the summer before. After completing his trading with the Indians, McQuesten returned to Stewart River as he had made arrangements to take Boswell upriver as far as he could. It was then that Boswell first told McQuesten about their exciting discovery. This deception greatly annoyed McQuesten who later wrote: ". . .it was wrong in his not telling the other boys as there was only five of them and they were all prospectors."

After travelling about 12 miles up the Stewart River McQuesten and Boswell encountered six men rocking on a bar. They had come in from Juneau that spring and had gone up the river after Boswell had come down. They were making $5 a day. McQuesten and Boswell had dinner with the men, but when the subject turned to mining, Boswell once again denied that he had found anything. The six had planned to go out in a few days, but after McQuesten revealed to one of them that the Boswell group had in fact found some exciting prospects, they decided to stay.

About 15 miles further the river became too shallow for the steamer to proceed. So, after caching their goods, McQuesten and Boswell continued in a canoe. At Steamboat Bar they met the other prospectors.

"I worked five days with them and made $250.00," wrote McQuesten. "There were fifteen men in the country that winter and they were all expecting to strike it rich." Later, one of the men mining Steamboat Bar gave an indication of just how rich it was. They had arrived just after the ground had thawed but with the river still frozen solid. Before the ice went out ". . .we had cleaned up $30,000. It was a regular thing for each rocker to clean up. . .to $300 per day."

News of the discoveries on the Stewart River soon reached the outside, and in the summer of 1886 a small gold rush started when about 100 men came in from Juneau. They climbed over Chilkoot Pass and worked their way down the Yukon River to the mouth of the Stewart, where, in a single season they recovered about $100,000 worth of gold dust.

To service these miners, McQuesten and Harper erected a new trading post there the same summer, and around it soon grew a 100-man village. Then, anticipating an even more active trade for the following year, McQuesten left for San Francisco to get supplies.

That fall, on the advice of Harper, Howard Franklin and Henry Madison decided to check out Fortymile River, about 100 miles downstream from the Stewart. Harper had found good prospects there in 1874, but had been deceived by the Indians and did not investigate further. Harper had always wanted to return, but never had the opportunity. Franklin and Madison decided it was worth a look, and after announcing their intentions at Stewart River, five newcomers agreed to accompany them for a more thorough examination.

At Fortymile the party found prospects on every bar, but nothing spectacular. Then, on September 7, 1886, it happened. "I left the camp and walked upstream about two miles," wrote Franklin. "I found a place where the bedrock was exposed, and in a crevice succeeded in getting out a shovelful of dirt. When I panned this I was surprised to find that it had much coarse gold in it. I hastened back to camp and showed the boys what I had got. We weighed my prospect and if I am not mistaken it weighed a half an ounce, or about $8.50 as gold went in those days."

Returning to the site, the prospectors were unable to locate more coarse gold. All were convinced, however, that Franklin's nuggets meant they were on the right track, so they continued upriver. When they again struck good prospects on another bar, they named it Franklin in honour of the discoverer. Franklin was not too impressed with the discovery, however, and after staking a claim, he and Madison moved a few miles farther up the creek. At this point they decided to return to the post at Stewart River for supplies and to "let the boys know that we had found coarse gold on the Forty Mile."

It was October, 1886, when Franklin reached Stewart with news of his discovery. It electrified the camp. Here at last were the elusive nuggets everyone was seeking. Abandoning Stewart River almost to a man, the miners followed Franklin back to Fortymile. Soon gold was discovered along the whole length of Fortymile and all its gulches.

This was exciting news for all concerned, but it created a dilemma for Harper. He knew that when news of this rich new discovery reached the outside, hundreds of miners would rush in. While this was good for business, it caused a serious problem: there was not enough supplies to feed the expected stampede. Harper would somehow have to get word to McQuesten so that he could substantially increase his order or there would be starvation in the Yukon. But how could he notify McQuesten? It was winter; the Yukon River was frozen solid, and all communication with the outside world was cut off. The nearest point of civilization was John Healy's trading post on the far side of the Chilkoot Mountains on Dyea Inlet. In between lay 500 miles of hostile wilderness few men had navigated in winter. Who would volunteer to take Harper's message?

Tom Williams, a prospector when he was not employed as a river-boat pilot for the A.C.C., volunteered. Williams had entered the Yukon by way of St. Michaels and had never travelled over the route he was now agreeing to tackle. Yet, despite warnings from friends that the journey was far too dangerous, and that there were no roadhouses where he could rest or replenish his supplies, Williams was determined to try.

Aided only by some crude maps and accompanied by an Indian boy who had never been over the route either, Williams loaded a mail sack on a dog sled and left Stewart on December 3.

The journey, as expected, was a most difficult one. In the dead of winter ". . .over the hummocks of river ice and the copses of fallen trees, through the cold jungles of the Yukon forests, and up the slippery flanks of the mountains" they trudged onward. Even before they reached the mountains their three dogs had died of cold, exhaustion or hunger, and Williams and the Indian boy, now out of provisions, were forced to eat them to survive.

Now on foot, weakened by cold and hunger, they clawed their way up the Chilkoot summit and straight into the teeth of a vicious blizzard. By the time they reached Stone House, so named from a large mass of rocks, Williams was too exhausted to continue. Digging a hole in the snow, the Indian fashioned a shelter into which they crawled to wait out the storm. Without food or heat, they shivered in their snow house for three days, during which time their faces, hands and feet became blackened by frostbite.

On the fourth day the weather abated only slightly, but they knew that if they were to have any chance of survival they must reach Dyea soon. With Williams too weak to walk, the boy somehow hoisted him to his shoulders and began the long descent. When the exhausted Indian could no longer carry Williams, he dropped him in the snow and staggered on alone. It appeared certain that both men would perish, but at Sheep Camp, a rest stop at the edge of the tree line, the boy suddenly came upon a group of prospectors waiting out the storm. They followed him back up the mountain and helped bring Williams down to Sheep Camp where he was revived with hot soup. The courageous Indian then borrowed a sled and dragged the barely conscious Williams the remaining 26 miles to Healy's trading post at Dyea. But it was too late for Williams. He died two days later without regaining consciousness.

Healy and the men gathered in the post were naturally anxious to learn what life-or-death mission had inspired this race over the Chilkoot Pass in the dead of winter. The Indian, knowing few works of English, glanced around the room. Seeing a sack of beans on Healy's counter, he grabbed a handful and flung them on the floor, saying: "Gold. All same like this!"

When news of the discovery on Fortymile River reached Victoria in the spring of 1887, about 500 people started off for the goldfields and the Yukon experienced its first gold rush. Although it is estimated that there was $200,000 taken out that season, the rest of the world was still blissfully unaware of the potential wealth buried in the Yukon Valley.

Up to 1886, the finds in the Yukon district were confined almost entirely to territory traversed by the headwaters of the Yukon River, embracing the White, Stewart, Pelly and Hootalinqua rivers. In that year, what may be called the middle division of the Yukon, extending from Fort Selkirk to the mouth of the Tanana River, was first opened up by the discovery on Fortymile River. Not long after this discovery, a few miners crossed the narrow divide which separates the headwaters of Fortymile from those of Sixtymile and discovered gold on Miller and Glacier creeks. The former had already been prospected three different times and given up as worthless, but it turned out to be the richest creek in the region and enjoyed that reputation for years.

For the next several years about 300 miners were at work in the Fortymile region during the summer. The town of Fortymile grew at the mouth of the river, but as the small steamer plying the Yukon could not bring in provisions enough to winter more than 100, the other 200 had to make their way out each fall. After the *Arctic* began to make regular trips on the Yukon from St. Michael in 1890, there were more provisions available and more men were able to winter in the Yukon.

In 1891, gold was discovered in American territory on the headwaters of Birch Creek, which flows into the Yukon about 40 miles below Fort Yukon. The initial discovery, which has already been described, had been made by Rev. Robert MacDonald 28 years earlier, but had been ignored at the time. When this information was relayed by McQuesten to two native Indians, Syrosca and Pitka, they set out to locate the gulch to which MacDonald had referred. Their discovery led to the founding of Circle City, on the banks of the Yukon, about 200 miles below Fortymile. Soon Circle City began to attract the old-timers and newcomers who had been unsuccessful on other streams and it quickly became the most important mining camp in Alaska, a reputation it would enjoy until 1896, its peak year, during which gold production exceeded $1,000,000. Then it was almost wiped off the map by the exodus to the Klondike. At the moment there still were not many gold seekers in the Yukon Valley. However, each year saw a few more enter the area after hearing about one discovery or another.

RABBIT CREEK

It was an insignificant little creek trickling through a moose pasture. Numerous gold-hungry prospectors had passed by the creek without giving it a second thought. But the discovery made here on August 17, 1896, would fire the imagination of men everywhere and trigger the greatest gold rush in history.

ARTHUR "Bad Luck" Harper had been the first prospector to enter the Yukon to search for gold. Since 1873 he had searched intermittently for the elusive metal but, although he found prospects in several areas, the big strike had always eluded him. Fate was unkind to Harper, who called the Yukon home for 24 years. During that time he prospected or tested nearly every mining district that later proved to be rich in gold, except for the Klondike. Almost exhausted by tuberculosis, Harper left the Yukon in August, 1897, on the eve of the greatest gold rush the world had ever seen. He died in Yuma, Arizona the following summer. He was 62 years old.

But Harper was not to be the only hapless soul who sought, in vain, the Yukon's golden riches. One of the most persistent, and, as future events would reveal, most unfortunate, was Robert Henderson, a lighthouse-keeper's son from Big Island, off the coast of Nova Scotia.

A rugged, earnest man with clear blue eyes, Henderson began his lifelong pursuit of gold while still a teenager. He had been a sailor for some years and had travelled the globe. Of an adventuresome nature, he sought gold more for the excitement than the financial reward. For Henderson, the challenge lay in the thrill of discovery, and the trail had led him to New Zealand, Australia, the Pacific Northwest, and finally, at 37 years of age, to the Yukon Valley. There, true to his adventuresome spirit, the six-foot Henderson ignored the already established goldfields at Fortymile River and Birch Creek. Instead, he turned his attention to the Pelly River. But there was no gold on the Pelly and, now broke, Henderson and two associates, Kendrick and Snider, drifted toward Sixtymile River.

When the trio arrived at the small settlement of Ogilvie,

located on an island at the mouth of the Sixtymile River, they found the ever smiling Joseph Ladue, a French Canadian, in charge of the trading post. Originally from Plattsburg, New York, Ladue had first entered the Yukon as a prospector in 1882. But when his mining ventures failed, Ladue decided to become a trader and entered into the service of Arthur Harper and LeRoy McQuesten.

After Harper and McQuesten separated in 1889, Ladue went into partnership with Harper. At this time Birch Creek, in Alaska, and Fortymile River were the two principal mining districts. But Ladue realized that his only chance to prosper was to grow with a new region. So, having faith that other creeks would be discovered as rich as Fortymile, he moved to Sixtymile where he and Harper built a trading post and sawmill.

Destined to become the founder of Dawson City, Ladue has been described as both an "enthusiastic advocate" of the Yukon and a "liar," depending, apparently, upon one's point of view. According to some, Ladue promoted the Yukon and the possibilities of new discoveries at every opportunity. Others, however, were less kind. They claimed he would lie or deceive to further his own interests. For telling so-called "lies" about the richness of Indian River, he had almost been driven from Fortymile by the irate miners.

Whichever the case, Ladue told Henderson and his associates they would find good prospects on Indian River, which joined the Yukon River about 20 miles below them. The fact that it was comparatively virgin ground was enough to arouse the adventuresome Henderson. His associates, however, were not as easily enthused. They had become disillusioned with the Yukon and decided to returned to Colorado.

After resting for a few days at Ogilvie, Henderson obtained a grubstake from Ladue and, with a new-found companion, started out for Indian River. Once there, they went upriver as far as a creek they named Quartz, continuing up it to the divide between it and what is now Hunker Creek. When provisions ran out the two men returned to Ogilvie.

After obtaining another grubstake from Ladue, Henderson returned alone to Indian River where he spent the winter of 1894-95 prospecting, mainly on Quartz Creek. To reach bedrock through the frozen ground, logs were piled up and set afire. This procedure had first been tried successfully by Fred Hutchinson at Franklin Gulch on the Fortymile River in 1887.

After the fire was extinguished, the thawed earth was removed as deep as possible, wherein another pile of logs was stacked in the shaft and set ablaze. This procedure was repeated as many times as necessary until the shaft was sunk to bedrock, where the largest concentration of gold was normally found. It usually required two men to mine a creek in this fashion in winter, during which as many as 30 cords of wood would be used. For a lone man, this was laborious and tedious work, but Henderson's only reward was a few colours.

Most prospectors would have been thoroughly discouraged by such meagre results, but not Henderson. In March, 1895, he prospected a large branch of Indian River named Australian Creek. If he had gone a little further up Indian River, he would have discovered the rich diggings of Dominion and Sulphur creeks. Instead, he was not only denied success, but at one point he suffered an accident which nearly claimed his life.

Henderson was prospecting near the head of the creek when it became necessary for him to cross. As it was during spring freshet, Henderson had to fall a tree over the creek to use as a bridge. To make the tree passable, its numerous limbs had to be cut off. While in the act of doing this, Henderson lost his balance. As he fell he impaled himself on the calf of the left leg, piercing it in such a way that he hung suspended from the limb. Although in terrible agony, Henderson nevertheless managed to swing himself up on the tree. He then struggled

McQuesten's two storey log building trading post at Circle City, Alaska. It also served as the post office.

back to camp where his wound confined him for 14 days.

Upon recovering, Henderson shot some moose and caribou, and from their hides, fashioned a boat with which to float down the Indian River. He then paddled up the Yukon River to Ogilvie, where he remained only long enough to obtain provisions. Then, with William Redford, he made his way back to Quartz Creek, where they ground-sluiced some of the top material off in preparation for next season's operations. When their provisions were exhausted, they returned to Ogilvie where, after waiting several weeks, Henderson was able to obtain a year's grubstake from Ladue. With fresh supplies, Henderson returned to Quartz Creek where he spent the winter prospecting alone.

In the spring of 1896, Al Day and a companion paid Henderson a brief visit and found him sluicing. Before they left, he showed them the $400 in gold he had already recovered. Altogether, Henderson would recover $620, which, for the time and effort expended, was not very encouraging. He then ascended Australian Creek, prospecting it and all its branches. His cursory examination revealed nothing and he returned to Quartz, which he ascended to its head. After crossing over a short, sharp divide, Henderson descended into the deep-cleft valley of a small stream flowing northward. Testing the gravel he found 2¢ to the pan, which was more promising than anything he had found previously. Encouraged, he named the creek Gold Bottom and decided to work it. Returning to Ogilvie for supplies, he induced four men, Ed Munson, Frank Swanson, Albert Dalton and an Italian named Liberati to accompany him.

☆　☆　☆

Meanwhile, on the bank of the Yukon River at Fort Selkirk, an individual who was shortly to play an important role in the future of the Yukon was quietly observing the sunset.

George Washington Carmack, or "Siwash" George as he was more generally known, had jumped ship in Skagway a decade earlier. As he packed over the Chilkoot Pass he became acquainted with two Indians named Skookum Jim and Tagish Charlie.

Skookum Jim was a full-blooded Tagish Indian and the brother of a Tagish Chief. He is described by Carmack as having "high cheek bones, hawk-like nose, and large, piercing black eyes, well nearly six feet in height, and straight as a gun barrel, powerfully built. . . ." He was also very strong, hence the name "Skookum." Tagish Charlie was described by Carmack as "a fine specimen of the Northern Indian, lean and lithe as a panther, keen in perception, and as alert as a weasel, the type of man to tie to in case of emergency." Others, however, were not as flattering. Tappan Adney, author of *The Klondike Stampede,* wrote that he was also known as "Cultus" Charlie, which meant worthless.

Carmack quickly became fond of his Indian companions and for the next two years the trio prospected the Big Salmon River and the Hootalinqua. "Jim was a whale with a rocker," Carmack wrote, "while Charley (sic) could handle a pick and shovel as well as any white man."

Carmack soon settled into Indian life and married Jim's sister Kate. At the moment, however, he sat alone trying to decide his future. Suddenly he reached into his pocket and removed a silver dollar, the only money he possessed, and flipped it high into the air. If it came down heads, he decided, he would return upriver; if it was tails, he would continue down river. It landed tails, so Carmack pushed his boat into the current and began to drift down river to Fortymile.

At Fortymile, Carmack was again undecided as to what to do, but that night he had a very vivid dream. "I dreamed that

The town of Ogilvie or Sixtymile was situated on Ogilvie Island, 20 miles downstream from the Stewart River. During the gold rush, Joe Ladue's large trading post, shown here, catered to the needs of passing miners.

(Above) The Taylor & Drury Store Ltd., at Fort Selkirk, in 1988. It was first established in 1892.
(Right) A view of some of the buildings being restored at Fort Selkirk.
(Below) Cairn marking Carmack's "Discovery Claim" on Bonanza Creek in 1988.

I was sitting on the bank of a small stream of water, watching the grayling shoot the rapids," he wrote in *My Experiences in the Yukon*. "Suddenly the grayling began to scatter and two very large King salmon shot up the stream in a flurry of foaming water and came to a dead stop in front of the bank where I was sitting. They were two beautiful fish, but I noticed that instead of having scales, they were covered with an armour of bright gold nuggets, and had $20 gold pieces for eyes."

The dream stirred Carmack so deeply that he was unable to get back to sleep, and as he lay there he tried to interpret its meaning. For a white man like Carmack, it should have been a clear indication to go prospecting. But Carmack had adopted to Indian life so well that he interpreted the vision as a sign that he should go fishing. He then purchased twine and set about building a large gill net. By the time it was completed, Carmack had decided that he would try his luck on the Tron Deg River about 50 miles upriver from Fortymile.

(The Klondike River had originally been given the name Tron Deg by Arthur Harper and Jack McQuesten who got the name from the Indians in the vicinity. In English, Tron Deg meant "Hammer-water" and was derived from the fact that local Indians "hammered" stakes across its mouth to divert salmon into their fish traps. It was a famous salmon river, and when William Ogilvie first passed it on September 1, 1887, the whole width of the river bed was staked and half a dozen families were camped there fishing. How it came to be called Klondike is unknown.)

On July 1, 1896, Carmack loaded his boat and headed for the Klondike River. After establishing camp, Carmack spread his net across the mouth of the river. Although the fishing turned out to be very poor, Carmack had such faith in his dream, he decided to stay. Then, near the end of July, Carmack

noticed three Indians approaching in a boat. As they neared his camp he recognised his brother-in-law Skookum Jim, accompanied with Tagish Charlie and his brother Patsy.

☆　☆　☆

Meanwhile, at Gold Bottom, the Henderson party had once again run out of provisions, and, leaving the others at work, Henderson started out for Ogilvie. As he travelled down the Indian River, Henderson found the water so low that his empty boat often grounded, and he knew he would never be able to return by that route with a full load of supplies. He believed, correctly, that Gold Bottom was a tributary of the Klondike River. So, upon obtaining his supplies, Henderson decided he would return by that route.

When Henderson reached Ladue's trading post at Ogilvie, there were about a dozen miners gathered there. Upon informing them that his party had recovered $750 from Gold Bottom Creek, which was the first gold ever recovered in what later became known as the Klondike District, they all headed overland accompanied by two horses loaded with supplies. At the same time, true to form, Ladue began spreading the news of a rich new discovery on Gold Bottom to anyone who would listen. The veterans were sceptical because of Ladue's past history, but many newcomers also set off in search of the new goldfields.

Loaded with fresh supplies, Henderson headed down the Yukon River. At the mouth of the Klondike he spotted Carmack, whom he had known for a couple of years, fishing with his Indian friends.

"There is a poor devil who hasn't struck it," he thought as he headed his boat ashore to inform Carmack about his discovery on Gold Bottom.

What exactly transpired during that brief meeting has always been opened to dispute. William Ogilvie, who served as surveyor for the Dominion Government in the Yukon for many years, interviewed the four principal individuals, Jim, Charlie, Carmack and Henderson at great length — some of them several times. In 1913 he wrote probably the most accurate recounting of the events in his book *Early Days on the Yukon.*

"As Henderson tells the story Carmac (sic) promised to take it in, and take his Indian associates with him, but to this Henderson strongly objected, saying he did not want his creek to be staked by a lot of natives, more especially natives from the upper river. Carmac seemed to be offended by this objection, so they parted. I have this story substantially the same from both Henderson and Carmac, the latter of course, laying a little stress on the objection of the Indians."

In his booklet *My Experiences in the Yukon,* Carmack states that, upon being informed about the discovery, he asked Henderson: "What are the chances to locate there, everything staked?" According to Carmack, Henderson eyed the Indians standing nearby, then replied: "Well, there's a chance for you George, but I don't want any damn Siwashes staking on that creek."

Although he did not know it at the time, Henderson's attitude and prejudice against Carmack's Indian companions would cost him a fortune. Jim and Charlie had understood every word, and as Henderson headed upriver, Jim angrily asked: "Wats matter dat white man? Him killet Inchen moose, Inchen caribou, ketchet gold Inchen country, no liket Inchen staket claim, wha fo, no good?"

Carmack calmed his companions by assuring them that it was a large country and they would find a creek of their own. But there was no hurry, first, it was agreed they would cut some logs which could be sold at Fortymile for $25 per 1,000 board feet, and Skookum Jim set of to check out the area for a possible source. Jim's search led him to a little creek called Rabbit that entered the Klondike River about a mile above its mouth. (Rabbit Creek had never been prospected before, although both Harper and McQuesten had hunted moose there.)

After locating some suitable logs a distance up Rabbit Creek, Jim began a careful examination of the creek bed to determine if they could be floated down to the Klondike. In so doing he found "colours" at various places in the gravel, and where claim 66 below Discovery was afterwards located, he found what he considered very fair prospects. However, when Jim returned to the fish-camp and revealed what he had found, it did not create very much interest.

About three weeks after Henderson's visit, Carmack decided it was time to check out the prospects at Henderson's Gold Bottom, and the three men, with a small pack of provisions, a shovel and a gold pan, set out early in the morning. Their route took them up the Klondike River to Rabbit Creek, which they then followed. Travelling up the valley of the creek through thick underbrush was tedious and fatiguing, and the mosquitoes tormented them relentlessly.

A short distance below where they afterward made their discovery, Jim panned some gravel during a rest break. His efforts were rewarded with a few cents in fine gold and two coarse pieces about the size of a BB shot. This was a fine prospect and Jim thought they should stake right there. After a brief discussion, however, it was agreed that they would continue to Gold Bottom, and if they found nothing better, they would return to stake Rabbit Creek. Jim and Charlie then asked Carmack if they should tell Henderson of their discovery, but Carmack suggested they reveal nothing until they could return to investigate further.

Carmack picks up the story: "The next morning we went up the creek panning here and there, getting a little gold in every pan. We passed one bench coming in from the south which we did not stop to prospect, but went up the other fork, which was afterwards called Eldorado, and turned out to be the richest creek ever found in the Yukon Territory. On this creek we also found some good prospects.

"After going up this creek a couple of miles I found the remains of an old campfire which had evidently been made by white men in the winter. Nor was I wrong; Joe Ladue told me afterwards that in the winter of 1884-85, while wintering at old Fort Reliance, he and some other men were up in that part of the country hunting moose. Little did they dream that winter night of the wealth that lay under the frozen ground they were sleeping on."

The party continued to the head of the creek and emerged on top of a ridge, which they followed until they reached the Dome, a high bald hill which stood at the head of a series of small creeks that radiated towards the Klondike and Indian rivers like spokes from the hub of a wheel. The view was spectacular, and Carmack's description shows he was not the uneducated, unrefined individual many people still believe.

"It was a glorious day. The valley bed lay like a beautiful Oriental rug, its rich colors tinted by the warm flood of golden light, projecting its rays into every nook and cranny, upon every living. tumbling, rushing stream coursing its way down the hillsides. The lower range of the hills on either side were crimson and purple and emerald green, all softened and blended into a maze-like tapestry. A great fringe of huckleberry and salmonberry bushes, interwoven with one another in

(Above) Carmack's Discovery Claim on Bonanza Creek in its early stages of development. Visible in photograph is the "Discovery Post" upon which Carmack recorded his claim on August 17, 1896.
(Left) George Washington Carmack.
(Below) Exterior of Bonanza Hotel on claim no. 60, 1899. The signs advertised Scotch and rye whisky, wine, liquors, cigars, meals and lunches at all hours. Note the telegraph pole which does not yet have wire strung through.

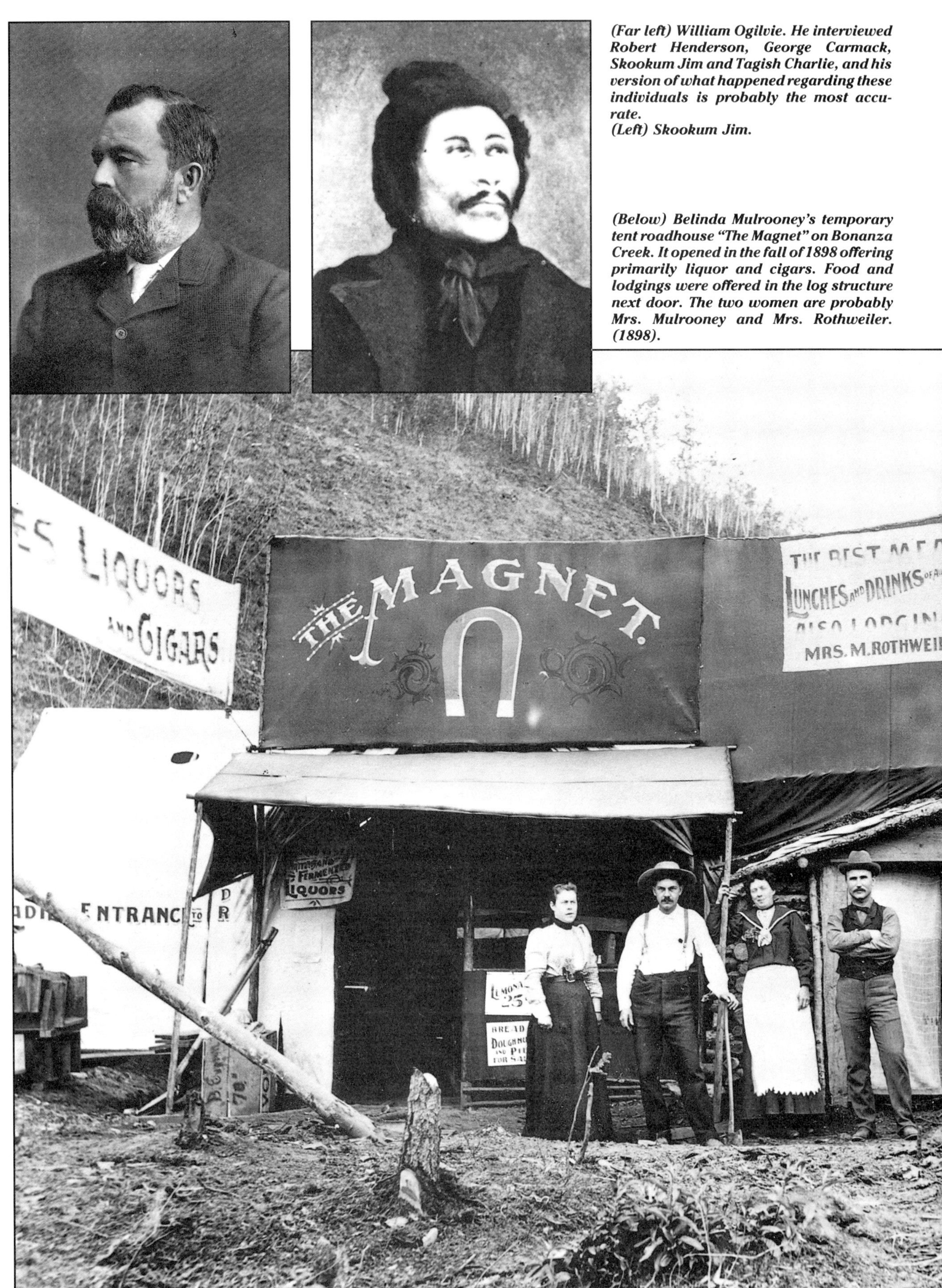

(Far left) William Ogilvie. He interviewed Robert Henderson, George Carmack, Skookum Jim and Tagish Charlie, and his version of what happened regarding these individuals is probably the most accurate.
(Left) Skookum Jim.

(Below) Belinda Mulrooney's temporary tent roadhouse "The Magnet" on Bonanza Creek. It opened in the fall of 1898 offering primarily liquor and cigars. Food and lodgings were offered in the log structure next door. The two women are probably Mrs. Mulrooney and Mrs. Rothweiler. (1898).

luxurious profusion, marked the lines of the foothills.

"From a small canyon just below us a wisp of smoke was rising, evidently from a camp fire which I at once concluded must be the camp of the Henderson party."

At this point, according to Carmack, there was some dissension among the small party. Jim, in particular, still resented the remarks made by Henderson on their previous meeting and did not want to venture further. After some discussion, however, Jim finally relented and the three men descended to Henderson's camp. This is Carmack's version of that meeting.

"There were four men there, Henderson, Swanson, Monson, (sic) and Dalton. 'Hello George,' said Henderson. 'You found us at last, eh?' 'Well yes, it was accidental. We found some good prospects in a creek over on the other side of that range and seeing your camp from up on that mountain we came around out of our way to tell you about it.' I then asked permission to try a few pans on their claim. He told me to go ahead, so I tried several pans of gravel, both on the surface and down in the cut, but I could not get as good a prospect as I got over on the other creek. I then showed him the prospect that I had saved and advised him to go back with me and locate, but he did not seem to be interested.

"As far as I ever heard, Henderson's claim never did show up over two or three cents to the pan. His childish, unreasoning prejudice would not even allow him to stake on the same creek with the despised 'Siwashes' so his obstinacy lost him a fortune."

Ogilvie's version of the events that transpired is somewhat different. In *Early Days on the Yukon,* he wrote that by the

(Above) Three miners posing with gold pans, shovels and pickaxes in front of their cabin on no. 5 Below Discovery, Gold Bottom, in 1898. In the foreground is cribbing for a shaft.
(Below) A panoramic view of the town of Gold Bottom at the junction of Gold Bottom and Hunker creeks, 1899.

time Carmack, Jim and Charlie reached Henderson's camp, ". . .they were nearly bare of provisions, and completely out of tobacco, a serious predicament for Jim and Charlie. Henderson, either through shortage himself or dislike of the Indians, or both, would not let them have any, though Jim and Charlie both assured me they offered to pay well for all they could get, which Jim was both able and willing to do. As they did not find any prospect approaching in value the ten-cent pan on Bonanza (Rabbit), they remained a short time at Henderson's camp, and made their way back to the head of the creek which first gave fame to the Klondike — Bonanza. Before they got down it their provisions were entirely exhausted, and as they prospected on the way down, and Jim was hunting for meat, their progress was slow; and their hunger was becoming acute, with exhaustion and weakness fast following."

Finally, Jim was able to kill a moose, then shouted to the others, who were still some distance away, to join him. While waiting, Jim took some meat to the creek to wash it. There, he ". . .found gold. . .in greater quantities than he had ever seen it before."

After the others arrived and they feasted on moose meat, Jim showed them the gold-laden gravels. For the next two days they panned and tested up and down the creek, satisfying themselves they had the best spot. At this point a dispute arose as to who should stake the discovery claim. "Jim claiming it by right of discovery," wrote Ogilvie, "and Carmac claiming it, Jim says, on the ground that an Indian would not be

Bonanza Creek claim. Millions in raw gold was taken out of Bonanza Creek following the discovery of gold there in 1896.

allowed to record it. Jim says the difficulty was finally settled by agreeing that Carmac was to stake and to record discovery claim, and assign half of it, or a half-interest in it, to Jim. . . ."

The following morning, after breakfast, Carmack wrote, "I went out into the center of the flat to a small spruce tree and blazed it on the up and down stream sides. With a pencil, I wrote on the up-stream side, this notice:

"TO WHOM IT MAY CONCERN:

"I do, this day, locate and claim, by right of discovery, five hundred feet, running up stream from this notice. Located this 17th day of August, 1896.

"G.W. Carmack.

"Then taking a fifty-foot tape line, which I had in my pack, we measured off five hundred feet up stream, as a discovery claim, then five hundred feet more, as one above discovery, for Jim. Then going back, I measured off five hundred feet for myself by right of location, then five hundred feet as two below discovery for Charley (sic). Then going back to a tall birch tree, standing on the bank near the point of discovery, I cut off a section of bark and wrote on it these words: I name this creek Bonanza. George Carmack."

The threesome then panned enough gold from the surface gravel to fill a Winchester rifle cartridge. Then, after a gruelling tramp through swamps and devil club thorns, they emerged at the mouth of Bonanza "feeling like human pin cushions."

Retrieving their boat, they pushed off for their fishing camp at the mouth of the Klondike River. They had travelled only a short distance when they encountered four men, Dan McGillivery, Dave Edwards, Harry Waugh and Dave McKay, wading upriver towing a boat. They had been told about Henderson's

strike on Gold Bottom by Ladue and were on there way to that location. Carmack smugly informed them that he had been to Gold Bottom and the prospects there were not good. He then showed them the gold he had recovered from Bonanza Creek and, supplying directions, suggested the four gold seekers would do much better there. Spurred on by the sight of the gold, the men lost no time in heading upriver.

No sooner had Carmack reached their fishing camp when two men were spotted coming down the Yukon River in a small boat. Headed for Fortymile, the two French Canadians would not even have stopped if Carmack had not hailed them in. Once again Carmack displayed the gold-filled cartridge and gave directions to the new discovery on Bonanza Creek. He then crossed the river to tell the exciting news to Edward Monahan and a man named Cooper.

Early the next morning, while Carmack and Charlie headed for the mining recorder's office at Fortymile, Jim returned to Bonanza Creek to watch over the claims. After recording the claims at Fortymile, Carmack headed for the most popular saloon. As expected, the saloon was crowded with miners from nearby creeks, most of whom were in town to secure winter outfits. After a couple of drinks, Carmack turned his back to the bar, held up his hand and said: "Boys, I've got some good news to tell you. There's a big strike up the river."

At first no one paid much attention to the news. Most were veteran miners who dismissed it outright as another scheme of Ladue to start a stampede which would benefit his trading post. Others held a prejudice against Carmack because of his long association with Indians and because he was not really a bona-fide miner. Even when he emptied the contents of the cartridge on the gold scales, most remained sceptical and just kept on drinking.

Then one curious miner examined the gold more closely and announced that it was different from any he had ever seen. Suddenly the room began to stir as each man in turn approached the bar to view the evidence. Carmack was telling the truth, and few bothered waiting for more details that the location of the new field, before slipping out of the saloon. The news soon spread throughout the town and virtually overnight, Fortymile was deserted. Soon the entire Yukon Valley was buzzing the name Bonanza.

Joseph Ladue, who had started for the mouth of the Klondike a short time after Henderson, was among the first to hear of Carmack's strike. He promptly staked a town-site at the mouth of the Klondike and was about to start for Fortymile to register it when he met a man who wanted some lumber. Ladue then forwarded his application by another party, and returned to his mill at Sixtymile. There he loaded up with nails, spikes, and lumber, and returning to the mouth of the Klondike, built a cabin and a rough 22x40-foot warehouse. These were the first buildings in Dawson, the name given to the new town by Ladue in honour of Dr. George M. Dawson, director of the Canadian Geological Survey.

During the early rush to Bonanza there were few old-timers that showed any interest. *They* claimed to know all about the Klondike, declaring it nothing but a "moose pasture." It was unlike any other place where they had seen gold. Some climbed the hills and walked along the divide until they could look down into the valley of Bonanza. Here many of they stopped and threw up their hands in disgust. Others who

Mrs. J. Lowe's Laundry on Bonanza Creek in 1898. Mending of clothes was "Free of Charge," but if you wanted your fortune told, it cost $1.

A panoramic view of Dawson City during the summer of 1898.

actually visited the creek, cursed and swore at those who persuaded them to come there. One old-timer who ventured up Bonanza as far as No. 20 above Discovery, where the last stakes were, remarked as he turned away, "I'll leave it to the Swedes." Another is said to have written on the stakes of No. 21: "This moose-pasture is reserved for the Swedes and Checakoes." (The Swedes were supposed to be willing to work the poorest ground.)

Louis Rhodes staked it right afterwards. Then, being ashamed of staking in such a place, told his companions that he would cut his name off for two bits. Rhodes tried to sell the claim for $250, but there were no takers. Reluctantly, and almost apologetically, he was forced to work the claim himself. In early October he struck pay dirt at the 15-foot level of his claim and promptly hired men to work for him. On November 23, they recovered a pan worth $65.30.

This was the first big pan of any importance, and the information spread up and down the creek like wildfire. According to *The Klondike Stampede,* when the news reached Fortymile, one veteran miner scoffed: "That's a lie. Louis Rhodes! When was he able to hire two men?" (The next summer Rhodes cleaned up $44,000.) "Next word came down that Ben Wall was getting two-bit dirt. 'Hell!' said Nigger Jim; I've known Ben Wall these 10 years, and he's the all firedest liar in the Yukon.' When they heard that (Clarence) Barry was getting $1 to the pan, they laughed. Klondike was a bunco — nothing but a bunco."

During this period, a Klondike claim was considered worthless. A half interest in one of the richest Eldorado claims was sold for a sack of flour, while a few thousand dollars could have bought up the entire creek from end to end.

Some of the prospectors who had provisions remained on Bonanza to prospect; most, however, returned to Fortymile, where their arrival coincided with the miners coming in from the diggings. For the first time, this new group learned about the strike on Bonanza. Among them was a Swede named Charlie Anderson. By the time Anderson reached the new diggings there was nothing left to stake and, after a fruitless attempt to reach a distant creek from which gold had been reported, he returned discouraged to Dawson. There he was approached by a gambler who offered to sell him No. 29 on Eldorado for $800.

"I'll take it," replied Anderson, who had taken out a considerable sum that summer from a claim on Miller Creek, at the head of Sixtymile River, and he weighed out the dust. The enterprising salesman went about boasting how he had played Charlie for a "sucker," only he wanted someone to kick him for not having asked for $1,200. As it turned out, it was the gambler who missed out on the fortune. When Eldorado began to "prove up," even Anderson could not realized the enormous value of his claim, from which he eventually recovered $400,000!

☆ ☆ ☆

On Gold Bottom Creek, Henderson and his partners were totally oblivious to the tremendous riches being mined just over the ridge. In fact, Bonanza had been staked into the 80s above Discovery, and Eldorado to No. 33 — or over three miles — before a party of miners crossed over the divide to Gold Bottom.

When Henderson asked them where they had come from, the men pointed over the hill and replied Bonanza Creek. Henderson knew immediately they were referring to Rabbit Creek. Upon being told that it was the greatest discovery ever made in the Yukon and that it had been discovered by Carmack, Henderson was devastated. He threw down his shovel and sat down on the bank, so sick at heart that it was a long time before he was able to speak.

Henderson always bitterly resented that fact that Carmack had never sent word of his discovery as Henderson claimed he promised to do if he found anything better than Gold Bottom. As a result, Henderson did not learn about the rich discovery, which was brought about through his labours and his

invitations to come to Gold Bottom, until it was too late. Nor did Henderson's ill-fortune end there. Prospecting a large fork of Gold Bottom, he made a discovery which yielded 35¢ to the pan. Staking a discoverer's double claim, he started for Fortymile to record it.

On the way he met Andrew Hunker and Charles Johnson who had staked No. 31 and No. 43 below on Bonanza. They told Henderson that they had made a discovery of $3 to the pan on the other fork of Henderson's "Gold Bottom" Creek, two miles below, on September 5. They told Henderson they thought he could not hold Discovery over their claim, and as their new discovery was apparently better than his own, he staked No. 3 above. This fork was first called Hunker's Fork of Gold Bottom, but as subsequent staking began at Hunker's discovery, the whole creek to its mouth was recorded as Hunker Creek, despite the fact that in July Henderson had written on a large tree at the junction of the creek with the Klondike River, "This creek to be known as Gold Bottom Creek." En route to Fortymile, Henderson stopped and recorded another claim on Bear Creek.

Upon reaching Fortymile, Henderson was told that a new mining regulation provided that no person could hold more than one claim in a mining "district," instead of being allowed a claim on each separate creek. There is no doubt that at the time Henderson drove his stakes he was entitled to either four or five claims. The law which was to deprive him of all but one claim came into force between the time he staked and the day he reached Fortymile.

Forced to make a choice, Henderson decided to record No. 3 above on Hunker. That winter, Henderson was laid up and unable to work due to the injury he had suffered at Indian River. The following spring, true to his nature, he ignored his claim and ventured 40 miles up the Yukon prospecting for new finds. He soon returned and proceeded to a large creek two miles below the mouth of Stewart River, and 11 miles up the creek subsequently named Henderson, made a discovery of 10¢ to the pan.

Returning to Dawson, Henderson boarded a steamer for the outside. Unfortunately, fate intervened again. Frozen in with the other miners at Circle City, he was under a doctor's care all winter. In order to pay his bills, it was necessary to sell No. 3 above Discovery on Hunker Creek for $3,000 — a mere fraction of its value.

In October, 1898, Henderson finally arrived in Seattle. During the journey, unsuspecting and trusting, he had been robbed of all the money he possessed — $1,000. His only remaining possession was the golden carpenter's ruler and myrtle leaves badge of the Yukon Order of Pioneers, of which he was a member. Pinning it to the vest of Tappan Adney, a totally disheartened Henderson said: "You keep this. I will lose it too. I am not fit to live among civilized men." Henderson then returned to Aspen, Colorado, where his wife and child lived. There he returned to work in the same mine where he had worked six years earlier.

When Carmack made the discovery on Bonanza Creek (actually, Skookum Jim made the discovery, Carmack stole the glory), Henderson's involvement was not clearly understood, and Henderson was not one to promote himself. Later, however, William Ogilvie bestowed upon Henderson some of the credit he so richly deserved:

"The Klondike was prospected for 40 miles in 1887, without anything being found, and again in 1893, with a similar lack of result; but the difference is seen when the right course is taken, and this was led by Robert Henderson. This man is a born prospector, and you could not persuade him to stay on even the richest claim on Bonanza. He started up in a small boat to spend the summer and winter on Stewart prospecting. This is the stuff the true prospector is made of, and I am proud to say he is a Canadian."

Probably of more satisfaction to Henderson, his peers, the miners, who knew the facts, always credited him with the discovery of the Klondike. "Siwash George," they said, "would be fishing yet at the mouth of the Klondike if it hadn't been for Bob Henderson." To that, I heartily agree.

QUEEN OF THE KLONDIKE

Her name was Kathlene Rockwell, but she was known to the world as "Klondike Kate." From obscurity in a small town in Kansas, Kate made her way to the Yukon during the height of the gold rush madness. In Dawson City, her performance as a dance-hall girl earned her fame and fortune. After a love affair with Alex Pantages ended in bitterness, Kate returned to Oregon.

KATHLEEN Eloisa Rockwell was born on October 4, 1876, at Junction City, Kansas of Scotch-Irish parents. Her father, John Rockwell, worked for the Missouri & Western Railroad, while her mother, Martha Murphy, was a waitress. When Kate was five, her parents divorced. A year later Martha married her divorce attorney, Francis Bettis, and, with Kathleen, they moved to Spokane Falls, Washington. There the family moved into a large house and lived in high style, with several servants and even a governess for Kathleen. Bettis became prominent in local politics, was soon elected to town council and became a judge.

Kathleen, a bouncy, energetic child, was a tomboy who liked to catch crayfish in the river with other kids. Warm-hearted, she was eager to help other people. Once, after a big fire destroyed part of Spokane Falls, Kathleen invited the homeless to come and live with her family. Many accepted the offer, which greatly angered her mother, but her stepfather was amused. The astute judge knew that the well-meaning intentions of his stepdaughter would gain him political points.

As Kathleen grew older, her desirability to young men opened up a happy world or picnics, parties, box socials, hay rides, and sometimes a jaunt in a buggy with a handsome young suitor. "Boy crazy," the gossips decided, and she did become an outrageous flirt.

This happy, irresponsible time came to an end for Kathleen when a stock market crash wiped out Judge Bettis' fortune. To make matters worse, Kathleen's mother had been losing money on her real estate deals. Complicating the financial situation was the fact that Frank and Martha had not been getting along for some time, but stayed together because of their wealth and social position. When Frank ordered Martha

to end her extravagant ways, she refused, and the judge sent her packing. The estranged couple then sold their properties to pay off their debts.

Martha operated a boarding house in Spokane until she received her share of the money from the sale of the Bettis property. Then Martha decided to take her daughter on a sea voyage to New York. The journey would be made by way of Valparaiso, Chile, where her son Morris, Kathleen's half-brother, was living. At Seattle, they found a four-masted sailing ship which was putting in at Valparaiso, but the captain stated that it was against company policy to carry passengers. In the end, however, he agreed to sign her and Kathleen on as "stewardesses."

After almost three months of visiting South American ports well off the beaten track, the ship sailed into the calm harbour of Valparaiso. As mother and daughter went ashore, Kathleen confided that she was engaged to a nice, young ship's officer. Her angry mother, in spite of protests from Kathleen that she was a big girl now, registered her wayward child in the Convent of the Sacred Heart. Perhaps the strait-laced, French-speaking nuns could keep her under control.

After a brief visit with her son, Martha decided to travel to New York alone and send for Kathleen later. However, once at sea, Martha's plans changed, and when Kathleen next heard from her mother, she was in England.

Meanwhile, as the only unmarried American girl in Valparaiso, Kathleen attracted numerous suitors. She had a fine time dancing with the lively, carefree Latin men, under the eyes, of course, of the glowering chaperon. They taught her Spanish dances, including the fandango, and encouraged her to smoke cigarettes by showing her how to "roll her own." Before long she had collected seven more diamond rings, including one from her leading suitor, the young attache of the Spanish Legation.

When Martha heard about the state of affairs, she set sail from England to New York, from where she cabled Kathleen to join her. The *Willie Rosenfeld,* anchored in the harbour, was bound for New York, but the captain said it was fully booked. However, when Kathleen learned that the first mate's wife decided to remain in Valparaiso, she convinced the officer to let her pose as his wife.

When Kathleen arrived in New York three months later, she learned that her mother had spent all her savings and was now sewing shirts for $4 a week. Kathleen was soon able to supplement that income by earning $18 a week as a chorus girl. Martha did not like the idea of her daughter living it up as a chorine, but, as Kathleen pointed out, she was now over 20 and old enough to live her own life.

In the Naughty Nineties, New York was an exciting place for a young lady. Before long, however, Kate yearned for a change of scene and accepted a job as a dancer in Spokane, her old home town, in a place featuring "continuous vaudeville."

The saloon-cum-theatre was not all it was cracked up to be, however. Kathleen's dancing act was only part of her role; she was also expected to use her feminine charms to get the customers to buy drinks, on which she received a percentage.

In time, however, Kathleen began to travel the Northwest looking for new opportunities. Eventually she worked her way to Seattle, which was then in the throes of the Klondike stampede. The waterfront was jammed with ships and supplies. On the wharves, eager crowds of miners, prospectors, traders, businessmen and adventurers jostled one another while thieves and pickpockets relieved them of their money and possessions. Saloons, dance halls and brothels competed for what was left.

After only two weeks at the People's Theatre in Seattle, Kathleen received an offer from the Savoy in Victoria, British Columbia. This was supposed to be a step up for the ambitious entertainer, but, as before, she was to be a "come-on girl," expected to hawk liquor to the men.

Every day Kathleen heard tall stories from rough-talking miners who had returned from the Klondike. The stories proved to be an irresistible lure to Kathleen, and she became determined to visit Dawson City.

In 1899, Kathleen and Gertie Jackson, her partner in a "sister" act, quit the Savoy. After a nightmarish trip on an over-crowded, foul-smelling steamer, the two girls reached Skagway. In the rambling collection of tents, shacks and false-front buildings, the pair saw a tough frontier town with muddy streets bordered by saloons, gambling parlours, bawdy houses and dance halls. Gertie took one look at Skagway, decided she had seen enough and returned to "civilization." But Kathleen was determined to continue on.

Hearing that there were jobs for dance hall girls in Bennett, Kathleen boarded a passenger train on the White Pass & Yukon Railway. But once again, the so-called theatre where Kathleen worked turned out to be nothing but a poorly-lit saloon with a small stage. For two months, accompanied by only a pianist, Kathleen sang and danced her way into the hearts of lonely, discouraged men who loved to talk to the friendly, warm-hearted girl. Her admirers paid tribute in a unique way. Nailed to the ceiling of one of the hotels they had spelled out her name, KATIE ROCKWELL, with champagne corks.

Kathleen soon tired of Bennett and wanted to press on to Dawson, where the real opportunities lay. This meant running the gauntlet of Miles Canyon and Whitehorse Rapids, five miles of treacherous whirlpools, rapids and rocks where boats were often capsized and more than 200 lives had already been lost.

In 1898, Supt. Sam Steele of the North West Mounted Police (NWMP) had laid down the law: "No women or children will be taken in the boats. If they are strong enough to come to Klondyke, (sic) they can walk the 5 miles of grassy bank to the foot of the White Horse. . . ." He also laid down rules for boats and pilots, and the penalty for noncompliance was a $100 fine.

Kathleen was able to make her way down Lake Bennett to Canyon City, the small town at the head of Miles Canyon, without difficulty. When she tried to obtain transportation through Miles Canyon, however, a young NWMP constable intervened. Kathleen tried argument at first, then turned on her charm. Neither worked.

Angry, Kathleen stormed back to town. A short time later she returned to the landing disguised in an old flannel shirt and a pair of overalls. With her hair pushed up under a tattered cap, she waited for the Mounties to be preoccupied elsewhere. Then, making her way through a crowd of men, she jumped onto a large scow which was just casting off its lines. A short time later the blunt-nose craft was caught by the current and shot into the canyon. The scow bucked and plunged wildly over the waves, while Kathleen, soaked from the cold spray, clung desperately to the railing.

After a short section of calm water, the scow shot through Squaw Rapids like a cannonball, dodging dangerous snags and whirlpools. As the strong current whirled the groaning

(Above) The Montreal-London Gold & Silver Development Co.'s supplies leaving Skagway, May 20, 1898.
(Below) The tent settlement of Bennett City surrounds the Hotel Portland and Dawson Hotel. After performing here for a brief time, Kate made her way to Whitehorse.

craft towards the rocks, Kathleen feared the protesting planks would be torn apart in the boiling cauldron of the rapids. Then the bow veered away from the chaos to bob through the last of the white water and emerge into a calm pool near the bank. Truly frightened by the experience, Kathleen was never happier to set foot on dry land.

Short of money, Kathleen was soon entertaining in one of the Whitehorse dance halls. One day a letter arrived from a girlfriend in Victoria advising her that a big theatrical company was being organised by the owners of the Savoy, and they planned on going to Dawson City in the spring. The owners wanted Kitty to play a soubrette. So, with Dawson City only a short paddle wheel trip away, Kathleen decided to return to Victoria.

The Savoy Theatrical Company was the largest vaudeville troupe ever to visit the Klondike. In the spring of 1900, 173 dancers, singers, actors, actresses, jugglers, comedians, back-up people, and a large ragtime orchestra, landed on the Dawson wharf.

The town, situated on the flats where the Klondike River joins the Yukon, was at its zenith with a population of close to 30,000 people. A disorderly, untidy town of tents, shanties, and log cabins, almost every other building was either a dance hall, saloon, hotel, or restaurant. On the waterfront, hundreds of boats were tied to wharves or beached on the muddy shore.

Seamstresses, maids, stagehands and carpenters got the company ready for the grand opening, and men streamed in from the creeks to view the gorgeous girls and hear the latest hit songs. On opening night, sourdoughs, merchants and gamblers packed into the Savoy. In front, the orchestra tuned up. Suddenly the cacophony ceased. A fanfare! The big stage exploded with light and action! The crowd cheered and whistled at the chorus line in flouncing skirts and spangled blouses. The girls wore saucy hats and carried bright-coloured parasols. They put on a sparkling sequence of dances and songs of the ragtime craze.

After a short drama in which the villain was deservedly hissed, Kathleen, nervous as she faced the noisy crowd for the first time, appeared on stage. Billed as "Soubrette Extraordinaire," she wore a huge, wide-brimmed hat with ostrich plumes dyed white and black *a la* Lillian Russell, and her narrow-waisted, lace-trimmed costume was in the mode of a Gibson Girl.

Singing to the accompaniment of a trombone, piano, cornets, and violins, the red-haired beauty laid them in the aisles. The men responded by tossing nuggets onto the stage as they bellowed for more. The show ended with the high kicks, leaps and twirling skirts of the chorus line in the naughty French cancan. Afterward, the floor was cleared for dancing and the girls of the Savoy Company, dressed in their finest, mingled with the men.

In those days, a dance hall could crowd in as many as 125 dances in a single night. From the stage, a caller or "spieler" urged: "Take your partners for a dreamy waltz." Usually, it cost $1 per dance and the girls received an ivory chip worth 25¢ as a commission for each dance. They tucked the chips into their stockings and cashed them in the next morning.

Many of the girls wore daring, low-cut costumes that showed an attractive bit of cleavage, available for intercepting any nuggets falling in that direction.

The waltzes were neither long nor dreamy. A miner had barely time to go around the floor once before the music stopped and the spieler shouted, "Belly up to the bar boys!"

Kathleen, in a white organdie with puffed sleeves, had danced many dances, and after a fast two-step ended up with her and her partner at the bar, she proposed a toast to Dawson and her new life.

Kate Rockwell, somewhere along the line "Kathleen" had vanished — became very busy and happy in her new stardom. In addition to the song-and-dance turns, she was featured in a fast-paced, roller-skating routine, and acted in plays. She also wrote skits and song lyrics, and often designed and made her own costumes.

Kate made good money. As a performer and dance hall girl, she received $50 a week, plus extra for her famous Flame Dance. Much in demand as a partner, the popular girl made hundreds of dollars dancing with the miners. It was a slow night when she did not take in $100. Visiting Vancouver in 1954, Kate recalled that she had been given a handful of nuggets worth nearly $200 from a sourdough who danced less than two minutes with her. Once, she said, a lonely man had paid her $750 for keeping him company throughout the evening. When pressed, she admitted to earning $30,000 per year.

On stage, Kate was an enticing temptress in pink tights and a glittering, rhinestone-studded costume. The Queen of the Klondike sometimes wore a collar studded with diamonds and gold nuggets. She possessed belts and bracelets made from $20 gold pieces, and paid $250 for her large, ornate hats.

Dance hall girls like Kate got more than a fair share of proposals and propositions, but unlike the girls of Lousetown, just across the Klondike River, they could select there own bed partners. In her first four months in Dawson, Kate estimated she had received over 100 proposals.

Some sourdoughs remembered her as "a good girl," and said, "she had a heart of gold." Others had no doubt that "She was a fast woman."

Kate herself, in later years, told reporters, "We were not vestal virgins. Far from it. We fell head over heels in love and made mistakes, but we supplied laughter and gaiety to lonely men."

Many people of those bygone days believe it was Kate's little-girl look that made her so popular and that she acted much younger that her years. At 24, she claimed she was 20. At any rate, she was happy, a headliner, and a wealthy young woman who lived in a private room with bay windows, above the lobby of the successful Savoy Theatre.

Kate was fortunate to be living in a town which, unlike Skagway, was relatively free from crime. Superintendent Steele of the NWMP had seen to that, for he had arrived in 1898 to find Dawson "a city of chaos" and set about to bring it under control. He borrowed soldiers from the Yukon Field Force and, with his NWMP detachment, clamped down hard on the criminal element. The Mounties dogged the heels of suspected felons and haunted the saloons and gambling halls. Steele planned for crooks to see redcoats every time they turned around, and concentrated on making life "unattractive" for them. Troublemakers got a blue ticket to leave the territory at once. They were shoved aboard a boat and told "to get the hell out of the country and never come back." Those who stayed after getting a ticket were sentenced to six months on the infamous Dawson woodpile, Steele's pride and joy.

Saloons, hotels, and dance halls had to pay expensive licenses and abide by strict rules. The gambling halls operated wide open, but Steele would shut them down for cheating or sharp practice. At midnight on Sunday, ragtime pianos ceased to tinkle, liquor was shut off, and gamblers left the tables.

The soiled doves of Dawson City had nothing to fear from the NWMP as long as their business was conducted in an orderly fashion. If the women acted discreetly, they would be treated with tolerance and courtesy. In this respect, it is likely that the police set a good example for the miners.

Perhaps Kate had this in mind when she told a Vancouver *Sun* reporter at a sourdough convention in 1954: "The sourdoughs had lots of respect for the girls. A decent lot of girls worked in the dance halls. It wasn't honky-tonk. the girls across the river didn't cut into our business, and we didn't cut into theirs. The dance-hall girls got a percentage on dances and got a salary besides."

One night Kate noticed a new waiter at the Savoy. Dark, husky and rather good-looking, the clean shaven Alexander Pantages was a dapper young man who liked to dress in the latest fashion. Pantages had migrated to the United States from Greece while still in his teens, and had joined the Klondike stampede to get his share of the gold. However, he soon found other ways of acquiring wealth. Pantages worked in Dawson as a dishwasher, saloon porter, handyman, and janitor. For a time he even held "sawdust rights" in one saloon — a monopoly in filtering sawdust from the floor in order to retrieve the spilled gold dust. He also sold coal oil to the miners, a job that paid him good money.

Kate and Alex got along well together for they enjoyed common interests: music, art, poetry, and the outdoors. Both were adventurers, both were ambitious, and both desired to make lots of money. It was not long before they became lovers.

Alex admired Kate's looks, education and intelligence, for he could neither read nor write English. He marvelled at her affluence and popularity. When his sweetheart drove through the streets in her buggy, she received homage in the form of enthusiastic whistles and yells from her fans. At $16 an ounce, her gold baubles were worth a small fortune. No wonder it suited Pantages to be at his most charming for her!

As Christmas, 1900, drew near, hundreds of prospectors left their isolated cabins on faraway creeks and headed for Dawson and the Yuletide celebrations. One of the prospectors who trudged across the frozen terrain was a 37-year-old Norwegian named John Matson who had a small claim on Matson Creek, 60 miles from Dawson. On Christmas Eve he entered the Savoy Theatre which was crowded with noisy sourdoughs drinking, gambling and having a great time. To the shy Norwegian, who did not smoke, drink or gamble, the cacophony was a shock to the senses. He felt out of place in the smoky, raucous hall, but he pushed his way past the faro, poker and roulette tables and sat down alone near the wall.

Eventually the show started, and the various acts came and went. Then, on centre stage, a tall, willowy girl appeared. Red, green and gold lights played over her curvaceous figure. As the music struck up, the attractive entertainer dropped a satin cape from her shoulders to reveal a long dress and train that contained 200 yards of chiffon. Turning slowly, the dancer wove the light cloth into a sea of fire, which threatened to flow over her and swallow her up. Now, with the music raising to a crescendo, the girl spun in and out of the long train of swirling chiffon. With the play of coloured lights on her shapely form, the dancer presented a dazzling sight of grace and beauty. As the girl melted to the floor, gossamer clouds of cloth settled around her still figure. The celebrated Flame Dance was at an end.

The hard-bitten miners cheered wildly. Some tossed nuggets and small pokes of gold gust onto the stage. In return, Kate threw them a bounty of kisses. After a short intermission, Kate appeared again, this time in a silver and white creation from Paris for which she had paid $1,500.

When the show ended, the miners and their dance-hall partners hopped and shuffled through a flurry or reels, two steps, schottisches and waltzes to the accompaniment of piano, drums, horns and violins. It was obvious to Matson that Kate was the most sought-after partner.

Kate had noticed the quit solitary figure sitting on the sidelines staring at her. Many years later she recalled: "I felt drawn to him and went over and took his hand and asked him if he wanted to dance."

But Matson could not dance, so Kate sat and chatted briefly with him. "I think I did most of the talking," she would later recall. Finally Kate rejoined the merrymakers and left Matson alone with his thoughts.

Like hundreds of other miners, the shy Norwegian had fallen in love with the Queen of the Klondike. Yet, although Matson occasionally returned to watch Kate perform, he never revealed his true feelings. After each visit, he simply took his secret back to his lonely claim on Matson Creek, where he worked a trap line in winter and mined gold in summer.

Meanwhile, Kate and Alex were making an effective team. She knew how to encourage her clients to order expensive wines. He, unobtrusive but attentive, kept up the supply of wine bottles for the clientele, often whisking away the used ones before they were empty. The skilful duo pulled in thousands of dollars each month. They continued to live together and soon were talking of marriage.

Using Kate's money, they opened up a new theatre called the Orpheum. With Kate as the headliner and Alex as entrepreneur, the Orpheum was a success. They brought in all kinds of fast-paced vaudeville acts which played to packed houses.

A bad period, however, was just around the corner. The Orpheum was burned out three times. Also, the Klondike boom had tapered off and many miners had left for the new strike at Nome, Alaska. The thoughts of Pantages began to turn to the States. With Kate's money, he thought he would like to try his hand at show business in the Pacific Northwest.

In the spring of 1902, Kate left for Seattle, and Pantages wound up the affairs of their theatre in Dawson City. On a trip to Victoria, Kate picked up a little nickelodeon, somewhat akin to a juke box, for $358, and also bought a machine for showing pictures that flickered when they moved and caused the viewers to have headaches and sore eyes. She added vaudeville acts to her show, including some of her own, and was doing well financially when Alex reappeared on the scene.

Instead of being pleased with Kate's latest success, however, Alex was extremely angry. He shouted at her and accused her of spending money foolishly with this combination of flickers and live acts. Kate defended herself and refused to give up her theatre. She enjoyed the work and made money, she said. She continued to live with Pantages, but he always brushed aside the topic of marriage.

Eventually, Alex came around to his mistress's way of thinking and bought a small, 10¢ movie-variety house on Second Avenue in Seattle. As Kate had done, he showed both flickers and vaudeville. It was the first theatre of what was to become the famous Pantages Vaudeville Circuit. Alex, in Seattle, and Kate, in Victoria, exchanged acts and two-reel pictures, until

Beautiful "Klondike Kate" Rockwell once wore a belt made of $20 gold pieces and a Parisian gown worth $1,500.

(Above) Two loaded barges docked at Canyon City dock of Miles Canyon Whitehorse Tramway Co. Mr. I.T. Mizony is seen making arrangements with a pilot to take the scows through the treacherous white water. It was here that Kate, disguised as a man, slipped pass the NWMP and jumped into a departing scow.

(Below) Lethal Whitehorse Rapids, where scores of boats were wrecked, their occupants drowned. The death toll was finally reduced when Supt. S. Steele stipulated that all boats must pass NWMP inspection.

she sold her enterprise for a good profit and used the money to back Pantages, who immediately bought another small theatre.

At some time in 1903, in order to earn more money for their theatrical ventures, Kate performed in variety halls in Galveston and Fort Worth, Texas, sending her considerable earnings back to Seattle to invest in what she considered to be *their* venture. She was happy to be on the road again, warmed by the applause of admirers. Alex, through a friend, wrote letters vowing his love and pleading for more money.

When Kate returned to Seattle almost a year later, she found a cool, remote Alex immersed in the business of vaudeville houses. Alex told Kate about *his* plans for a chain of theatres throughout the Pacific Northwest.

Kate helped him with the Crystal Theatre, and sang and danced on the same bill as a young talented violinist, Lois Mendenhall, whom she had met back in Texas. Restless as ever, Kate accepted bookings in other theatres and went on tour in her old home town of Spokane, where she was now a celebrity. While there, she received a letter from a friend in Seattle advising her that Alex had just married Lois Mendenhall.

Kate's dreams of marriage were shattered and she now had a deep, empty feeling, as if, in her allegiance to Alex, she had wasted the best years of her life. Unable to bear the thought that Alex and his new wife were now benefitting from all the work and money she had poured into the theatrical enterprise, Kate became depressed and was unable to sleep. She became unkempt, began to drink heavily and lost interest in her work.

Eventually, Kate got her excessive drinking under control and decided to fight for her rights. On May 25, 1905, almost two months after the marriage, Kate Rockwell filed a breach of promise suit for $25,000 in the superior court at Seattle. The Seattle *Daily Times* headlined: USES HER MONEY AND THEN JILTS THE GIRL.

The story of the Klondike love affair followed. Kate, said the article, claimed that the Pantages' success story was due to her backing. She had supported him in Dawson when he was out of work and had supplied him with luxuries when they lived together. In the States, she had travelled with Pantages as his wife, on her money.

At first, Pantages denied that he had ever known Kate, but later admitted that she was a "former acquaintance." By this time, he owned a number of theatres right across the U.S.

As the tedious suit dragged on, Kate lost heart and settle out of court for less than $5,000. She had not gained the revenge she sought, but did succeed in embarrassing her former lover by giving unflattering stories about him to the press.

Sad at heart, Kate returned to Dawson City. But the gold rush was over and the glitter and glamour gone. After four months, Kate found her heart was not in her work and returned to the Pacific Northwest to do vaudeville and act in dramatic stock. Still overwrought and unsettled, she wandered over the countryside, working without conviction but knowing, for her, the show had to go on.

One day Kate got a letter from Edith Neil in Fairbanks, Alaska. Neil, nicknamed the "Oregon Mare" because she had a laugh like the neigh of a horse, told Kate that a small hotel and rooming house was for sale if she wished to return to the Northland.

Kate, reunited with her friend, bought the hotel but lost it when a fire swept through Fairbanks. Discouraged, she turned to dance halls in the Alaskan city to build up her bank account. For the first time since being jilted by Pantages, she found that she really enjoyed being on the stage once again.

Going back to the States, Kate revived her Flame Dance. As before, the act caught the public fancy and Kate Rockwell was once more a big name on bill boards and theatre marquees.

Then Kate teamed up with Jimmy Ray, a champion roller skater, in an act in which the pair performed fancy dance steps and acrobatics on roller skates. Despite Kate's frequent falls and injuries, the dazzling routine made them a top attraction. But the bodily stress and strain eventually proved too much for Kate, and the act broke up. Returning to the less demanding song-and-dance bookings, a tired, depressed, lonely and unhappy Kate once again sought solace in a bottle.

Finally, on the verge of a nervous breakdown, a doctor told Kate to find a less stressful lifestyle. Heeding his advice, Kate moved to Bend, Oregon in 1910. After a time she moved to Medford, where she ran a boarding house for about a year. But vaudeville and wanderlust was still in her blood, and she was soon performing in variety halls on the west coast.

In 1914 Kate acquired, sight unseen, a god-forsaken 320-acre homestead in Bend. Despite the despair and isolation of the place, Kate plunged into her ranch chores with enthusiasm and energy. She had never been afraid of hard work. Folks marvelled at the sight of this vivacious lady dressed in one of her dancing costumes, with expensive jewellery and high-heeled shoes, carrying rocks, grubbing sage brush and cutting her own wood.

In 1915, at the age of 39, Kate married Floyd Wagner, a strapping, 20-year-old cowboy. Despite the age difference, the couple were reasonably happy for a time. Floyd lived on Kate's ranch and helped with the cattle. The new Mrs. Warner did her share of the chores, and was especially good at haying.

When Floyd enlisted in the army in 1917, Kate found that she was unable to manage the 320-acre spread by herself, and put it up for sale. With the proceeds, she bought a small convalescent nursing hospital in Prineville. Ten months later she sold it for $4,000. She put the money into a cafe, with the idea that she and Floyd would run it when he was discharged from the army.

When Floyd returned in 1918, however, the arrangement failed to work out. Within a year, after many quarrels, the Warners separated. Even before enlisting, Floyd had accused his wife of being wild and unfaithful. Now she hurled similar charges at him, and complained that he had beaten her up.

In 1922, Kate got an uncontested divorce and once again took the surname of Rockwell. At this time, she inherited money from her mother's estate, but soon squandered it and had to work as a waitress in cafes and logging camps. Moving down to Los Angeles, she found only part-time work at a low rate of pay, and, in dire straits, went to the mansion of Alex Pantages to hit him up for a loan. He gave her $6. Shocked and angry, Kate tramped the streets of the big city until she found a job as a waitress and saved enough for train fare to Oregon.

Back in Bend, Kate worked as a cook or waitress in small cafes and earned enough to renovate a two-storey house she had bought. Kate lived less than two blocks from the headquarters of the Bend Fire Department, and when a fire occurred in town, she soon arrived in her battered car with coffee for the volunteer firemen and a bottle of liquor in case any of them needed "first aid."

Kate soon enjoyed the same kind of love and respect from

the firemen as she had commanded among the sourdoughs in the Klondike. The men did not care what the proper ladies of the town might think, nor did they worry about Kate's "shady past." Instead, the firemen showed their appreciation by making Kate a lifetime honourary member of the department. It was a "love affair" that continued until her death.

Many people in Bend called her "Aunt Kate," for they remembered her nursing sick people during the influenza epidemic of 1918. Also, in hard times, she fed hoboes and unemployed men from her own meagre finances.

Others, however, criticized Kate's projects as a means of getting publicity. Indeed, at times she appeared determined to get her name into the newspapers. Frequently, she was accused of meddling in politics. Most, however, found it difficult to deny her good works. In one case, she had taken care of a quiet, unemployed little accountant named William Van Duren, who was almost blind from cataracts. Somehow, Kate raised the funds to take him to San Francisco to have the necessary operation. Afterwards, Van Duren was able to work again.

In 1929, Kate received a subpoena to appear as a character witness for the prosecution against her former lover, Alex Pantages, who had been indicted for the statutory rape of a 17-year-old dancer. At the trial, Kate enjoyed all the media attention, and benefited financially from photographs and interviews. Once again, she was in the limelight and she made the most of it by feeding stories to the press about her dazzling past in the old Klondike days.

Kate was never called as a witness against her former lover, who was found guilty and taken to jail to await sentencing. (The decision was appealed and two years later, Pantages was set free.) After the verdict was in, Kate sold the story of her life with Alex to the Los Angeles *Evening Herald.* The story, with pictures from her dance hall days, was printed on the first page. Returning to Bend with a load of photographs and clippings, Kate told her friends that Pantages got just what he deserved.

Nearly three years later, in his isolated cabin, John Matson read the Los Angeles newspaper with Kate's picture and an account of the Pantages trial. The little trapper had never forgotten that Christmas Eve in 1900 when he had watched the Flame Dance in the Savoy, performed by a radiant beauty with golden-red hair. She had asked him to dance and he had talked to her!

After many days, Matson finally finished a letter and hiked in to Dawson to post it. "I have always been in love with you, Kate, all these years," he wrote. "I never had the courage to tell you before. I have heard that life has not been too good for you. You have had lots of hardships. I would like to take care of you. I would like the right to take care of you as my wife."

Thus began a strange romance that lasted for two years.

(Opposite page) The Palace Grand Theatre, formerly the Savoy, in 1988. It was here that Klondike Kate entertained the gold miners of the Klondike gold rush. Her private room was behind the right bay windows.
(Below) St. Andrew's Night in the Savoy Theatre, Nov. 1899. The building has now been totally restored.

Klondike
Visitors
Association
DAWSON CITY
GASLIGHT FOLLIES
DIAMOND TOOTH GERTIES
R

At first, Kate could not recall the little Norwegian. On May 8, 1931, however, she replied, "Yes, I was the Kate Rockwell of the Xmas night in the Savoy." She went on to state that she was indeed experiencing hard times, and "I am trying to pay for a little home for my old age."

Later letters referred to the hardships she was having during the depression and thanked Matson for "the money you sent." (Matson is said to have sent Kate $20 per month from his trapping and mining efforts. Matson also established a bank account in her name.)

On October 26, 1931, Kate wrote, "I rec'd a letter & pass book from the bank in Vancouver a few days after yours. It is going to be a relief to pay up my small bills. I just can't tell you how much I appreciate your kindness — but some day I can show you."

Her suitor, now frozen in and far from the nearest post office, would not be able to correspond with Kate for months. At the end of 1931, she wrote to ask John what his intentions were. Would he send for her in the spring or had his feelings changed? "I get to wondering if you will send for me and let me go with you to Matson Creek."

During 1932, Kate became worried when she did not receive a letter from John. What had gone wrong? "Were the fotos so terrible or was it something I wrote in my letters?"

When there still was no reply, Kate's letters grew stiff and strained. She then addressed a registered letter to Matson in care of the Bank of Montreal in Dawson. In it, she stated that their romance was "just a foolish dream." If the letters meant so little, she said, "You could at least have said you didn't care to hear from me." Kate threatened to go away from Bend.

After a year in the mountains, Matson came out to Dawson and found a pile of Kate's letters waiting. He wrote at once to reassure her of his good intentions, and she immediately sent back a letter expressing her relief that he had not "changed his mind."

In the spring of 1933, Matson took his second trip to the "outside" in 35 years. At the age of 75 he was a strong, wiry little man. The first thing he did was buy a new suit for his rendezvous with his sweetheart in Vancouver.

Kate, a grey-haired 57, was still slender and gracious. In her, Matson saw the beautiful, vivacious dance hall girl he had fallen in love with over 32 years earlier. After the little trapper had overcome his shyness, the two talked for a long time in a hotel lobby. They were married in Vancouver on July 14, 1933. Matson's dream had been realized at last, for he had taken the Queen of the Klondike as his wife. As for Kate — she was enjoying the glow of the spotlight once again.

For their honeymoon, Mr. and Mrs. Matson made a sentimental journey to Dawson City. Although they received a warm homecoming, Kate noted that the town was no longer the Paris of the North. With its boarded-up windows and ruined buildings, it appeared more like a ghost town. The old Orpheum Theatre, once owned by her and Alex, was deserted and locked up, but the caretaker agreed to let the Matsons go inside.

For some time the new Mrs. Matson sat alone and silently communed with the ghosts of the past. She recalled the uproarious male laughter, the soprano chatter of the girls, the plink of the rinky-tink piano, and tried to remember what she had looked like when she had been the Darling of Dawson.

The Matsons had told the press that they would live in Dawson, but after a time Kate returned to Bend without Johnny. "No quarrel," she told her friends. "It was just that

This photo of Klondike Kate was taken at Dawson in 1900.

we both knew I couldn't live in a cabin miles away from the town and Johnny couldn't live anywhere else."

Kate made excuse after excuse not to return to live with her husband in the Klondike, and John stayed at his cabin, mining and trapping. He never went "outside" again. Perhaps, like many prospectors, he was hoping to make the big strike. Besides, he said he hated to live in towns. Their tenuous marriage was barely held together by infrequent letters. Kate's friends found the relationship hard to understand.

Year after year, when John came out of the back country into Dawson, Kate was there waiting for him. These partners in a strange marriage stayed in different hotels and then, after a few days, returned to their respective homes. Some sourdoughs viewed these goings on with a jaundiced eye and speculated that Kate's visits were timed to pick up her husband's poke. Others said that Kate may have suspected that her Johnny had a sizable cache of gold hidden out in the hills.

One old timer spoke with some bitterness: "Matson was in love with 'er. 'e was a short little man who talked with no one. She just took 'is money and 'is furs."

Matson continued to send his wife money, gold, and furs. During the Second World War their only contact was by letter, with the little Norwegian travelling long and dangerous miles to post his missives.

Meanwhile, Kate's fame continued to spread. She sold interviews to newspapers and she lent her name and photos to advertising and promotional schemes. For most folks, she was

This photo shows Klondike Kate, on right, with another Savoy Theatre entertainer, Lillie Edgerton. It was taken in Dawson City on July 10, 1901. Also seen in the photo are their three dogs, Tex, Nellie and Smithie.

a reminder of the Naughty Nineties and the days of the wild frontier. With her nugget jewellery and bright, flowery hats, Kate was good copy. She always carried a pack of Bull Durham cigarette tobacco and her own brand of blue, paper match books. On the door of her car was lettered: KATE ROCKWELL.

In the early 1940s, Kate was called to Hollywood to help write and advise on a film with Ann Savage in the role of Klondike Kate. There, she mingled with stars like Marlene Dietrich and Cary Grant, and her old friend, Marjorie Rambeau, the Dawson City girl. Right off, she tangled with the producers about the authenticity of the picture. "Imagine," she laughed, "it showed a train going to Dawson."

Kate failed to make any money from the picture. When it was released, she said, "I don't recognize anything in it that happened to me!"

For her, the title "Klondike Kate" came to be regarded as a trademark, and she sued at the drop of a hat any person or persons who, in her estimation, took liberties with her name. She sued the National Broadcasting Company and co-defendants Fibber McGee and Molly for $450,000 because they made fun of her as a gambler's daughter on a radio program and held her up to ridicule. When a New York publishing company printed a detective story about a girl called "Klondike Kate," the "real" Kate claimed libel to the tune of $575,000. But, following her usual pattern, she settle out of court for a smaller sum.

In her correspondence of 1945, Kate got Johnny to promise to spend the winter with her in Oregon, and even bought a small house. In furnishing the home, she hurt her back, a condition which was to plague her for the rest of her life.

When a letter from her husband arrived in April of 1946, it began: "My dearest wife. . .I am so tired after this trip. . . ." He failed to sign the letter.

A worried Kate waited until October before flying north to Dawson City amid international headlines. There, Joe Sestak, a trapper, broke the sad news. He had found the body of the old Norwegian in his cabin; it had been partly devoured by wolverines. The old miner and trapper had had a long, productive but lonely life, living for almost half a century with the dream of a beautiful dance-hall girl — a dream which was turned into fragments of reality by an exchange of letters and a few fleeting visits. He was 83 years old.

Under Kate's instructions, John was buried in the middle of the flower bed in front of his humble log home. Kate made arrangements for a tombstone to be placed there later on. It was to be engraved with these words; He rests in the Yukon Hills he loved.

Except for his mining claim and $1,600 in a Vancouver bank, the old man had left Kate little in terms of wealth. Kate retained his mining claim for a long time, and when she let it go, Joe Sestak re-staked it to preserve it. For, because of Kate, the little miner had become a legend in the North.

At a sourdough convention held at the Hotel Vancouver in 1948, Kate was accompanied by her new husband, W.L. Van

Duren. He was the unemployed accountant whom she had helped to regain his eyesight back in the early 1930s. That September, she went back to Dawson to settle her former husband's estate.

Kate attended sourdough conventions in Vancouver in 1951 and 1954. During the latter visit, she walked with a cane. A reporter wrote: "The frail, little old lady told me she'd seen probably $1,000,000 slip through her fingers in a few years at the turn of the century."

In the same year, Kate flew to Los Angeles to appear with Groucho Marx on his television show. Despite her serious back problem, she kept on the move by making public appearances.

Once in awhile, the Van Durens returned to the High Desert — to the country that Klondike Kate loved. They visited her old homestead where the old shack still stood, and there they

(Opposite page, top) The bar in the lobby of the Palace Grand Theatre in 1988.
(Opposite page, bottom left) The Palace Grand had elegant rooms for its performers. This bedroom was once used by Klondike Kate.
(Opposite page, bottom right) This sitting room in the Palace Grand was once occupied by Klondike Kate, whose picture is seen on the wall.
(Right) Exterior view of the Dawson City post office in 1988.
(Below) Klondike Kate is shown driving the only tandem carriage in Dawson on Dominion Day, 1901. The Dawson City post office is in the background.

picnicked. In the evening, she watched the flaming sun set in the west — a sight that still gave her such an emotional lift. When the sky darkened and the air grew colder, the Van Durens drove quietly back to Bend.

On February 21, 1957, Kate died in her sleep at her modest house in Sweet Home, Oregon. She was 81. Magazines and newspapers throughout the U.S. and Canada revived the old dance-hall stories of the gold stampede and the tale of her strange romance with the shy, little trapper-miner, John Matson.

A month after her death, Klondike Kate's last testament to the North, a poem entitled "My Will," was read at the sourdoughs' annual banquet and dance in the ballroom of the Hotel Georgia in Vancouver. A special poem written by Robert Service, still alive in France, was read along with Kate's.

Her poem began:

And all that I can leave you
Are memories of the past
The dreams we dreamed together
That were too sweet to last.

In the fifth verse, Kate forgave the people who had maligned her:

To the ones who bandied gossip
Tore my heart with two-edged words —
I leave my full forgiveness
To combat bitter words.

At the banquet, 200 copies of the poem were handed out to the sourdoughs.

In accordance with Kate's wishes, on a cold autumn day in 1960, with snow covering the mountain tops, her ashes were scattered over the High Desert. They drifted with the wind into the sagebrush on the old homestead.

(Above) Klondike Kate in 1948. Note the gold nugget necklace.

(Opposite page, top) This photo of Klondike Kate is from the scene of "Searles and Rockwell" that made such a hit with the Seattle messenger boys.
(Right) A photo of Klondike Kate as she looked in 1941.
(Below) The Discovery Claim on Matson Creek in 1917. John Matson spent most of his life mining and trapping along this creek which, except for his annual trip to Dawson for supplies and once to marry Klondike Kate, he never left.

GATEWAY TO THE KLONDIKE

Described by the legendary Sam Steele of the North West Mounted Police as "the worse hell on earth," Skagway was wide open and brawling. Here, the notorious Jefferson "Soapy" Smith and his gang of ruffians terrorized the thousands who were headed for the Klondike goldfields.

ESTABLISHED by a man of vision a full decade before the Klondike gold rush began, Skagway was the so-called "easiest gateway to the Golden North." When Sam Steele arrived in Skagway on February 14, 1898, the town already had about 5,000 inhabitants, but, reported Steele, its "...population increased every day; gambling hells, dance halls and variety theatres were in full swing. Soapy Smith, a 'bad man,' and his gang of about 150 ruffians, ran the town and did what they pleased; almost the only persons safe from them were the members of our force. Robbery and murder were daily occurrences; many people came there with money, and next morning they had not had enough to get a meal, having been robbed or cheated out of their last cent. Shots were exchanged on the streets in broad daylight, and enraged Klondykers (sic) pursued the scoundrels of Soapy Smith's gang to get even with them."

The site of Skagway was preempted by William Moore and his son Bernard in 1887. Born in Germany in 1822, William Moore began sailing aboard schooners in the North Sea by the age of seven, and was operating a towboat service on the lower Mississippi by his early 20s. After fighting in the Mexican War he pursued the siren call of gold — first to California, then Peru, the Queen Charlotte Islands, back to California, then to the Fraser, Cariboo, and the Cassiar. He once owned and operated, among others, the Ss *Grappler* for the Stikine River trade. It was destroyed by fire in 1883.

Four years later, Moore's fortunes had hit rock bottom. With the end of the Cassiar gold rush, he was bankrupt, and his Victoria mansion and five steamboats were auctioned off to satisfy creditors. But while Moore was down, he certainly was not out, for he never took it as a guarantee that the current

(Above) Gold rush stampeders landing at Skagway in August, 1897.
(Below) Broadway, Skagway's main street, in 1897, with Clancy's Hotel shown at right.

state of his financial affairs were irreversible.

Meanwhile, in March, 1887, sons Bernard and William had been lured into the Yukon Valley when news of a rich gold discovery on Fortymile River reached Victoria. Sensing the possibilities, Captain Moore also turned his attention northward, becoming a member of the William Ogilvie survey party. On August 12, while young William remained at Fortymile, Bernard encountered Ogilvie's survey party at the mouth of the Pelly River and was reunited with his father.

Captain Moore decided to return upriver to the coast with son Bernard and his party, and after transferring 400 pounds of his outfit to their boat, they set out. Bernard kept a diary-style narrative of his experiences in Alaska and the Yukon, and in 1968, 49 years after his death, the information was published in a book titled *Skagway in Days Primeval.* Bernard wrote that, ". . .on their way upriver, after bidding the Ogilvie party good-bye; my father told me of his trip through a pass leading from a little bay called Skagway, about four miles or so south of Dyea, through which pass he and an Interior Indian called Stick, or Skookum Jim, picked their way through to Lake Bennett in the month of June. It took them seven days, however, for there was no trail of any kind and travelling was very hard most of the way."

When Moore reported his discovery to Ogilvie at Lake Bennett, Ogilvie immediately named it White Pass in honour of Sir Thomas White, Minister of the Interior at Ottawa. Captain Moore was excited by the prospects of this new pass, which he felt would divert the early spring travellers. He also related that Skagway was accessible by large ocean steamers at all times of the year and that it offered safe anchorage. Captain Moore was determined to erect a wharf and take up land at Skagway Bay, then cut a trail through the White Pass.

On October 21, 1887, William Moore and son Bernard landed at Skagway Bay. "Here," announced William, "we will cast our future lots and try to hew out our fortunes." And with that statement father and son located the most suitable site for a wharf and began cutting trees for log cribs. "We remained there for two months," wrote Bernard, "cutting timber and taking soundings of the entire bay to ascertain the depths of the water, with a view of putting in a wharf. We also paced off and made notes for a location of one hundred and sixty acres of land."

This was Captain Moore's last gamble. If he was right and the next big gold strike was in the Yukon Valley, the best jumping-off point for the White Pass, entrance to the Yukon, was right where he built his cabin on the wooded flat land at the head of the bay. The property would be worth a fortune.

In preparation for what was to come, William went to work blazing trails through the pass and building a wharf that extended a mile out over the tidal flats. Except for Healy's & Wilson's Trading Post at Dyea, Moore's homestead at Skagway was the only other permanent dwelling in the region. But the comparative solitude would not last long. By the time George Carmack, Skookum Jim and Tagish Charlie hit the jackpot on Rabbit (later Bonanza) Creek in 1896, Captain Moore was ready. The news created great excitement throughout the civilized world and sparked the greatest gold rush the world has ever seen.

The first boatload of stampeders arrived in idyllic Skagway Bay on July 26, 1897. From Victoria, Seattle and other points south, every crazy craft that had previously been condemned was now pressed into service for the new goldfields. Each disgorged hundreds of passengers, large quantities of supplies, mules and horses. Soon the beach was covered with their equipment, supplies and animals, and, as trees were being cut down to make way for tents, the town of Skagway began to take shape. In their frenzy for the yellow metal, however, the newcomers paid no attention to the old man who met them as they came ashore.

By August 12, the population of Skagway had swelled to the point that a committee was elected to oversee construction of the booming settlement. Frank Reid, later to earn a prominent place in Skagway history, was appointed town surveyor, and a $5 registry fee was assessed of those who wanted to live on one of the newly laid out 50-by-100-foot lots. Lumber was unloaded on the beach and the foundations for buildings were begun.

Broadway, the single, muddy main thoroughfare, was overloaded with men and animals. Along its rude boardwalk sprang up a blacksmith's shop ($5 a horseshoe), a tent drugstore, a restaurant (with "MEALS" written on the seat of an old pair of hanging trousers), and four saloons — the Bonanza, Grotto, Nugget and Pack Train.

Throughout all of this activity, Moore continued to protest his ownership of the land, but no one paid any attention. Then it was realized that the cabin Moore had built almost 10 years earlier, and in which he and his wife continued to live, was right in the middle of one of the new 60-foot-wide streets. Moore was summarily ordered to move. Angrily, he refused, but after a physical confrontation with the committee on his doorstep, he realized he had no choice. Moore then commenced a lawsuit against the town for reimbursement of his land. The court action took four years, but in the end Moore won and was awarded 25 percent of the original value of all lots. By this time, however, Moore hardly needed the money; he had already sold his wharf for $175,000, a sizeable fortune in those days.

As the summer of 1897 turned to fall, still the stampeders swarmed into Skagway. Hundreds of boats of all sorts dotted the bay and the beach hummed with activity. "A nest of ants taken into a strange country and stirred up by a stick" was how naturalist John Muir described the scene; a scene he personally deplored after knowing the setting in its natural state.

Five miles away, the town of Dyea, jumping-off point for the Chilkoot Pass, was developing in much the same way. Dyea, however, was destined to be a fairly peaceable frontier town, while Skagway was in for some tough times.

Skagway's problems resulted in large part because of inadequate preparation for the Klondike stampede by the United States government. This was in sharp contrast to the Canadian government which, as early as 1894 had sent out Superintendent Constantine to Fortymile River to investigate complaints of rowdy behaviour from American miners. Based on Constantine's report, it was decided that he, with Inspector Strickland, Assistant-Surgeon Wills and 20 non-commissioned officers and men should be stationed in the territory. In 1897, shortly after the gold rush began in earnest, the Canadian Minister of the Interior travelled the White Pass route to view the situation for himself. Later that year 57 North West Mounted Police (NWMP) were deployed to maintain law and order. They constructed outposts on the White Pass and Chilkoot summits for the collection of customs. "Each station was provisioned for six months, had machine guns, and a supply of ammunition."

The Americans, on the other hand, handled Skagway badly.

(Left) An exterior view of Jeff Smith's Parlor in Skagway in 1988.
(Opposite page) The famous Pack Train Inn on Broadway Street, Skagway.
(Below) William Moore's original log cabin still stands. It was the first building built in Skagway.
(Bottom) This Skagway bar scene featuring "Soapy" Smith was photographed in Jeff Smith's Parlor.

RIVER
JEWELRY
CHEVROLET

Except for vigilante justice, law and order was virtually nonexistent right from the outset. The tone was set early when a Frenchman was caught stealing from a cache on the White Pass trail in August. Wrote Pierre Burton in *Klondike:* "Again a committee was elected to deal with the offence, and deal with it they did, lashing their prisoner to a pole before his tent and, as he screamed for mercy, pumping him full of bullets. For three days his bloody cadaver hung suspended as an object lesson in summary justice." With almost no law enforcement officers on the American side of White Pass, Skagway was a brawling, wide open town where might was right and anarchy prevailed.

Then, in late October of 1897, as though this seething hellhole was not violent enough, Jefferson Randolf "Soapy" Smith stepped ashore with five companions.

"Soapy" Smith had earned his nickname by selling bars of soap for $1 to the gullible on the street corners of Chicago, Pittsburgh and other cities. Smith enticed passers-by to purchase his soap by announcing that some of the wrapped bars contained a $20 bill. However, slight of hand ensured that only his shills got the bars with the money.

Smith was in Denver, Colorado when news of the Klondike gold rush reached him. With a small band of hard-boiled con men, pickpockets, gamblers and swindlers, Smith went to Seattle where he boarded the Ss *City of Seattle* in the fall of 1897. Smith had already checked out most of the coastal towns before determining that lawless Skagway was his type of place.

Mrs. Harriet Pullen, a widow who ran a small boarding house near the waterfront, was among the first to see Smith standing on Skagway's main street corners expounding the virtues of his soap.

"Soap, soap — the miracle cleanser — soap, the heaven sent purifier. Men, next to Godliness is cleanliness, and I give you this nugget-like, sweet-smelling soap, for just a dollar a bar!" Occasionally, a yell of delight would be heard as someone unwrapped their bar to discover a $50 bill. These lucky individuals were invariably members of Smith's gang; only rarely were strangers allowed to win.

When Smith tired of peddling soap, he switched to the old shell game. In the beginning, people were tolerant, seeing little harm in Smith's activities, and his games flourished. But Smith was a twisted soul, a genius in the art of fraud and villainy.

Smith and his cronies set up their headquarters at Clancy's Saloon where their well organized operation soon included mugging, picking pockets and otherwise stealing anything they could get their hands on. In addition to outright theft, various cons and swindles were employed to fleece unsuspecting and unsophisticated cheechakos.

Smith constantly took on new recruits, and soon gangs of hardened criminals were flocking to Skagway. Many, like Joe Palmer, Chinamen Yee, Turner Jackson, Frisco Red, Tom Candy, George Wilder, Doc Baggs, Slim Jim Foster, Charles Bowers, Old Man Tripp and others, were from San Francisco's tough Barbary Coast. Smith's men were everywhere; on the docks greeting each arriving steamer in the guise of public-spirited citizens; in the town posing as business leaders; in the churches, posing as the clergy; even on the lonely mountain trails, posing as returning miners.

"The town was soon dotted with bogus business premises erected by Smith," wrote Pierre Burton in *Klondike,* "or by the men under his protection, for the purpose of fleecing the Klondikers. There were a Merchant's Exchange, a Telegraph Office, a Cut-Rate Ticket Office, a Reliable Packers, and an Information Bureau — all complete shams — to which the suckers were steered."

Smith's Telegraph Office was a brilliantly conceived con that bilked ignorant and gullible stampeders by the hundreds. For, although Skagway did not have telegraph connections to anywhere in 1898, hundreds paid $5 each to send messages to loved ones back home before leaving Skagway for the Yukon. Adding insult to injury, Smith always made sure they received a bogus reply within two to three hours. Naturally, it came collect!

Smith tried to keep himself personally aloof from the dirty deeds of his cronies, disavowing any and all knowledge of such crimes. The true two-faced scoundrel that he was, he would loudly raise his voice in support of tighter law enforcement after some particularly revolting crime. He also maintained a high profile by providing for widows, paying for funerals and even taking in stray dogs, while he continued to associate with some of the most prominent and supposedly respectable citizens of the town, including the deputy marshal.

Sam Steele, NWMP Superintendent, who first visited Skagway on February 14, 1898, described the town as "little better than a hell on earth." He, along with other members of the force, spent many nights in Skagway on their way to and from the Yukon; but as a Canadian lawman, he was powerless to intervene.

"At night," wrote Steele, "the crash of bands, shouts of 'Murder!'cries for help mingled with the cracked voices of the singers in the variety halls; and the wily 'box rushes' (the so-called 'actresses') cheated the tenderfeet and unwary travelers... In the dance hall the girl with the straw-colored hair tripped the light fantastic to a dollar a set, and in the White Pass above the town the shell game expert plied his trade and occasionally some poor fellow was found lying lifeless on his sled where he had sat down to rest, the powder marks on his back and his pockets inside out."

Arctic explorer Henry Toke Munn, passing through Skagway on his way north, wrote: "For the six nights I slept in Skagway there was shooting on the streets every night. At least one man was killed that I know of and probably others."

Englishman Alexander MacDonald commented that "There was no law whatsoever; might was right, the dead shot only was immune to danger."

"Hold-ups, robberies and shootings are part of the routine," reported a news dispatch.

As the months passed, Smith's actions became more callous and revolting. In March, 1898, Constable Rowan and Andy McGrath were slain in cold blood. Rowan was hurrying to get Doctor Whiting for his wife who was about to give birth, when he and McGrath were called into Rice's Variety Theatre, a saloon, to settle a dispute. Unknown to the two men, Fay, the bartender, was waiting behind the door with a gun. Without warning or provocation, Fay shot both men as they entered. They died instantly before a horrified crowd.

Soapy, of course, claimed no knowledge of the incident, but his henchmen rescued Fay from the hangmen at the last moment and spirited him out of town on a boat heading north. Smith then took up a collection for Rowan's wife and child, raising several thousand dollars.

The following month, after the tragic avalanche on the Chilkoot Pass, Soapy's men rushed over to the site where, posing as rescue workers, they stripped the bodies of rings, watches, money or any other valuables.

Skagway's notoriety soon spread far and wide, and by the summer of 1898 thousands of stampeders were bypassing Smith's domain for Dyea. This, of course, greatly concerned the founding fathers. The White Pass & Yukon Railroad was already started and Skagway was to be the terminus; crime could not be allowed to take over the city. Tensions were running high.

Meanwhile, Soapy Smith was becoming increasingly enamoured of the image he wanted to project to the world. When the Spanish-American War broke out on April 24, 1898, Smith immediately formed the National Guard of Alaska, opening a military office in a tent and recruiting men to serve in the Philippines. On May 1, he organized a demonstration and marched at the head of a two-block parade while cheering thousands lined the route.

But even as Smith swept Skagway along in this avalanche of patriotism, the members of his gang were carrying out their elaborate fleecing operation on gold-seekers returning home to serve their countries.

July 4 arrived and Smith was still flying high. With the main streets of Skagway gaily draped in bunting and the Governor of Alaska in attendance, Smith, riding a beautiful grey stallion, led the Independence Day parade.

But the character of Skagway had changed and opposition to Smith's way of doing things was not going to die down. By that summer of 1898, Skagway boasted a population of about 15,000, tradesman, restaurateurs, merchants and professional people who had established businesses, built homes and sent for their families. They wanted safe streets, schools for their children and reliable officials who would uphold the law.

When J.D. Stewart, a miner from Dawson, arrived in town with $2,800 in hard-earned gold dust, combustible Skagway was just waiting for a spark.

Stewart disregarded warnings that he should have his gold

(Left) Frank Reid and attendants at Bishop Rowe Hospital, Skagway, shortly before his death.
(Centre left) Frank Reid's grave in Skagway's gold rush cemetery.
(Below) Jefferson "Soapy" Smith, dead, July 8, 1898.
(Bottom) Some original 1898 buildings in Skagway in 1987.

locked in the hotel safe until his departure, then compounded his folly by allowing himself to be convinced by a couple of "gold-buyers" that the best price to be had for it was over at Jeff Smith's place. All too soon, the confused Stewart was back on the street minus his gold and unable to say who had stolen it.

Deputy Marshall Taylor received the news of Stewart's loss with a lack of concern bordering on total indifference. He even went so far as to suggest that Stewart should go back to the Klondike and get some more.

Stewart was irate, and as he stormed about town telling the story of the theft to anyone who would listen, the town merchants became uneasy. They realized that if word filtered back to Dawson that the first of the returning gold miners had been robbed in Skagway, other miners would avoid the town like the plague. This created a strong anti-Smith sentiment as crowds on the street openly discussed ways of getting Stewart's gold back. Soon a vigilante group had been formed.

In the face of such opposition, some of Smith's men began to get cold feet, but Smith stuck to the story that Stewart had lost the gold in a fair game of chance. He then issued a warning to his men: "I'll cut the ears off the first man who makes a move to give it back."

A citizen's meeting, first assembled at Sperry's warehouse, had to be adjourned twice due to confusion and infiltration by Smith's men. Finally it was agreed to gather at the end of William Moore's wharf. To prevent infiltration this time, four men, including Frank Reid, stood guard to identify each person who passed.

Billy Saportas, a newspaper reporter who doubled as a spy for Smith, sent him an urgent note; "The crowd is angry. If you want to do anything do it quick."

Smith, who uncharacteristically had been drinking since late afternoon, decided it was time to act. "I'll drive the bastards into the bay," he said, arming himself with a derringer, a .45 Colt revolver and a .30/30 Winchester.

As Smith stormed towards the dock, a dozen of his men followed at a distance of about 25 feet. Behind them was a sizeable crowd of onlookers. When Smith reached the wharf he was confronted by Reid. "You can't go down there, Smith."

Mrs. Pullen, one of the eyewitnesses, describes what happened next. Suddenly Smith "lunged at Reid, striking him a wicked blow, full in the face, with the butt-end of his Winchester. At the same time he screamed nasty insults at Reid, for he had always violently hated him.

"To defend himself against a second vicious attack, Reid grabbed Soapy's gun, shoving it to one side, and with his free hand he grasped for his own revolver. Tearing it loose from its holster he took quick aim at Soapy and fired, but, unfortunately, the hammer clicked on a blank cartridge. This certainly was bad for Reid! It gave Soapy Smith just time enough to turn his weapon and level it straight at Reid, who, by now, was taking another quick aim.

"For a few brief seconds both fellows glared fiercely, holding the bead on each other. Then, all at once, simultaneously, their guns spurted fire! To us, who were standing near, it seemed there was only one extra-loud blast. When the smoke cleared, there they lay, the two of them. Soapy Smith sprawled in a pool of his own blood — stone dead — shot through the heart! A few feet away, face down, gushing blood all over the place, lay Frank Reid. Quickly we turned him over and saw a horrible wound in his groin.

"He was still conscious when we carried him to Doc Whit-

ing's. He was calm — told us not to worry — said he'd soon recover. But twelve days later he died in awful agony. It was a terrible shock, for he was very popular in these parts. We lost a real hero that day."

With the death of Smith, an era had ended.

In the aftermath, Skagway went wild. Residents combed the town, rounding up key members of Smith's gang and ordering suspected members out of town. A U.S. Army detachment was rushed down from Dyea to restore order and stop lynchings. When calm prevailed, Skagway was finally on its way to becoming a genuine town and a decent place to live.

The new deputy marshal, Si Tanner, maintained the new law and order, and the previously hamstrung town council got down to attending to the needs of the community. To raise money for such items as schools and fire-fighting equipment, taxes were levied on Skagway merchants for the first time. In addition, fund-raising events were held and voluntary contributions solicited.

Life settled down to normal, or as close to normal as was possible in a northern gold rush town in the summer of 1898.

Clayton's outfitting store did its usual booming business, supplying miners with everything from shovels to underwear, and all along State Street, loaded pack trains and wagons still moved in a steady flow. Anderson's hardware and Anzer's shoe repair, side by side on State Street, were always busy, and the drugstore on the corner of Main and State continued to sell out of citronella whenever a north wind blew in clouds of mosquitoes.

At the corner of Broadway and Main, Rice's Pack Train tavern did a thriving business all day long, and in the evening, Lee Guthrie's gambling establishment on Main hummed with activity, as cheechakos and sourdoughs alike tried their hand at poker, blackjack, dice, roulette and other games of chance. Across the street at the Palace Theatre, Theodore Price and a six piece orchestra entertained a spellbound audience.

In the Dutch Kitchen on the southeast corner of State and Main, Dutch-costumed Eileen served up a dinner of sauerbraten (occasionally made of deer meat) for 50¢, about twice the going rate for similar fare further south.

Through the last part of 1898 and on into 1899, the character of Skagway continued to change.

Work was proceeding on the White Pass & Yukon Railway, connecting Skagway with Whitehorse, 110 miles northeast. The railway office workers, track-laying crews and their families, created a new and different boom for the town.

The Debating Club and Literary Society held regular meetings; the Tennis Club was formed, and the Women's Christian Temperance Union deplored the evils of drink. Construction began on McCabe College, Alaska's first stone building, financed by the Methodist-Episcopal Church. Skagway had become civilized.

By the turn of the century, the Klondike gold rush was over, and the miners, packers and gamblers who had crossed the streets of Skagway melted away. Although the town's population shrank to a few hundred almost overnight, it was spared the fate of many gold rush settlements and never became a ghost town. Instead, Skagway survived to become a respectable port with respectable citizens — with one of the most fascinating histories of any town, anywhere. Today it is that very history that contributes to its economic well being, as thousands of tourist travel there by car or cruise ship each year. Skagway may never again experience the rambunctious, boom town status it once had, but its future seems assured.

WHITE PASS & YUKON RAILWAY

The perils and hardships of carving a railroad through solid rock, over an icy mountain pass, sometimes in the nightmarish cold of an Arctic winter, made the completion of the White Pass & Yukon Railway an almost unbelievable accomplishment.

ON July 16, 1897, the *Excelsior,* of the Alaska Commercial Company, steamed into the harbour of San Francisco and came to her dock near the foot of Market Street. Aboard were about 40 prospectors who had wintered on the Yukon River. As they walked down the gangplank they staggered under the weight of valises, boxes and bundles filled with gold. The following morning the local papers printed the news of the *Excelsior* and her $750,000 in gold dust, along with the sensational story that the richest gold strike in North American mining history had been made on Bonanza Creek in the Yukon.

On July 17, the *Portland,* of the North American Transportation and Trading Company, arrived at Seattle with 60 miners and $800,000 in gold, confirming the report that the discovery surpassed anything ever before found in the world. Seattle and San Francisco papers plunged into the story with sensational fury.

But this was only the beginning. During August, September and October, steamer after steamer brought back men laden with golden wealth, until $2,500,000 had been put into circulation. Within a year some $5,600,000 had been extracted from Bonanza and Eldorado creeks alone.

The response to all this gold excitement was instantaneous and overwhelming, touching off a global gold rush to the Klondike. Countless men, women and children, mesmerized by the prospect of instant and easy riches, swamped the docks of San Francisco and Seattle seeking passage north. All manner of vessel, whether sea worthy or not, was quickly pressed into service.

On July 21, a Seattle despatch described the madness that was sweeping the west coast: "The good ship *Portland. . .*sails

(Above) The White Pass & Yukon Railway excursion train climbing from tidewater to the summit of White Pass. It is shown here passing the face of Slippery Rock.

(Left) On July 21, 1898, the first train to ever operate in Alaska ran out four miles to the end-of-track and returned back to Skagway. WP&YR engine No. 1 was also the first engine in Alaska. Renumbered 52, it is now on display across the street from the town's railroad depot.

(Right) Old engine No. 52 at the railroad roundhouse before the fire.

for Alaska tomorrow at noon. She will carry every passenger and every pound of cargo that she has the ability to transport. The *Portland* has booked for this passage 50 first-class and 98 second-class passengers. Fifteen hundred passengers are booked for Alaska for the overland passage. Every available steamer is full. The steamers *Queen, Mexico, City of Topeka, Al-Ki,* in rotation, will sail by August 5th, to be followed by the *Willamette, City of Kingston* and *City of Seattle,* pressed from service elsewhere."

The returning *Excelsior* was also booked to its full capacity, and 10 times that number were turned away. Even from Victoria and Vancouver, every steamer that could be pressed into service was preparing to deliver gold-crazed prospectors north.

During the earliest days of the rush, almost everyone headed for Dyea, where John J. Healy had established a small trading post in 1884. Although Dyea lay at the head of the only practical route into the interior, via Chilkoot Pass, it initially had no wharf and no deep water harbour. Because of this, ships were forced to anchor about a mile off shore. From there, perishable supplies were lightered in flat-bottom scows and small boats and taken to the water's edge where they were unceremoniously dumped on the tide-flat. All such items that would float were simply thrown overboard to be carried ashore on the in-coming tide. Horses, cows, sheep, dogs and other animals were simply backed off the ship, and forced to swim in the icy water.

On shore, every wave deposited supplies helter-skelter on the beach. To complicate matters, material taken ashore in boats was unceremoniously mixed with the tide-born supplies. With no companies as yet established to move these supplies from the shoreline across the mile of muddy tide-flat before the receding tide carried it back out to sea, it was every man for himself. Utter confusion reigned as prospectors scurried about in knee-deep mud, their task complicated by the fact that the supplies had not even been sorted. Tons of materials littered the shore, the tide was fast approaching, an no one even knew where to begin looking for their supplies. Grown men actually sat and cried like babies when they lost their battle with the sea and were forced to watch helplessly as salt water soaked into and destroyed everything they had purchased with their life's savings.

Those who were successful in retrieving their supplies then encountered freezing rain, snow and bitter cold, and there was no food or shelter except what they had carried with them. Most agonized as they viewed the towering, snow-capped mountains that barred their way, and despaired at the realization that they were still 650 frozen miles from their ultimate destination.

Those who could afford it, and elected to do so, returned on the same ship they had arrived on. Others, either lacking the return passage, or truly afflicted by "gold fever," pressed on with almost fanatical determination despite all the difficulties. And they would require every ounce of determination they possessed, for, if scaling the Chilkoot Pass was not bad enough, each man was required to carry enough supplies for one year — about a ton — and there was no transportation available except their own two feet.

It would take several days of canoeing and hard packing just to reach Sheep Camp from Dyea. From there, almost three miles straight up, Chilkoot Peak stood high and forbidding. In the distance, silhouetted against the snow, miners "...looked like hundreds of black ants carrying loads almost as big as themselves as they pushed on up the cold, hostile mountain."

Edward Lung, who was in the vanguard of the Klondike stampede, described the ordeal that he and thousands of others faced daily. "On and on we climbed. It was an arduous, dangerous trail all the way to the top. From the thousand feet at a place called 'The Scales,' it was almost perpendicular. The Indian packers had chiselled out steps in the frozen snow, which helped a little, but it was dangerous and slippery, testing the stamina and grit of every one of us. It was like climbing an icy stairway to hell."

Waiting at the summit was the North West Mounted Police (NWMP). No one was permitted to pass without a year's supply of food and essentials. Because a man could carry only about 70 to 100 pounds per trip, each gold seeker had to scale Chilkoot Pass not once, but as many as two dozen times or more.

Those who could no longer endure the hardships slid back down the icy slopes and left for home, cursing the madness that had driven them north. Some of the less fortunate died on the trail; but most pressed on with unbelievable, almost superhuman strength.

The Indians, who had once barred access to the Chilkoot Pass to everyone, were now profiting greatly from the packing of supplies. But they were far from popular with the miners. One prospector who passed through Dyea in 1896 described them as "...some of the dirtiest-looking Indians on the face of the earth," adding that they were lazy, unreliable and charged exorbitant prices. Their total disregard for contracts, and their inclination to abandon supplies anywhere, anytime, without the slightest provocation, soon opened the way for competition.

Healy & Wilson were the first to capitalize, augmenting their regular business by offering a horse-packing service from Dyea to Sheep Camp. As the demand for freight services increased, some individuals conceived schemes for transporting goods over the summit faster and easier. The first of these was put forth by a Swede named Peterson in 1895. Peterson's plan was to establish a "Sealskin Sled Tramway" to the summit. To accomplish this he sewed numerous large sealskins together into the shape of little boats, and then sewed heavy canvas sides on them with lashing cords. Ten sleds, each about two feet deep, were constructed. Peterson then placed heavy poles from the foot of the trail to the top of the summit, connecting them by a system of endless ropes, blocks and pulleys.

Peterson's concept was simple, though impractical. He would place five sleds at the upper end and five sleds at the lower end. By filling the top five sleds with snow, he was confident that, as they slid down the slope, the weight and gravity would be sufficient to lift the bottom five sleds, loaded with miners' supplies, to the summit. But the project proved to be a dismal failure and was promptly abandoned.

Among the early stampeders who landed at Dyea was a Boston capitalist named Thomas Nowell. Sizing up the situation, he announced that his recently incorporated Dyea-Klondike Transportation Company would construct an electrically-powered tramway to carry freight over the Chilkoot Pass. The lower end of the tramway would be connected to the company's wharf at Dyea by freight wagons and stages.

A short time later the Alaska Railroad & Transportation Company revealed plans to construct a competing tramway to the summit, this one gasoline-powered. While these two tramways were being launched, a third was being organized by a group of Tacoma businessmen. Incorporated on October 13, 1897, as the Chilkoot Railroad & Transport Company, with Hugh C. Wallace as president, its list of investors included bankers, transportation officials, and an assortment of industrialists.

Meanwhile, Dyea was no longer the only town vying for supremacy as the principal port of entry to the Klondike. In 1887 Capt. William Moore and his son had preempted 160 acres of land at Skagway Bay, four miles south of Dyea, and had built a cabin and started construction on a wharf. Moore's interest in the area peaked when he discovered the White Pass earlier the same year. Moore was convinced that the White Pass would ultimately be the main route to the interior. Unfortunately, Moore had been unable to obtain the financial backing necessary to develop his scheme. For a decade it had fallen into limbo, and there it lay until news of Carmack's electrifying strike on Bonanza Creek set off a flood of humanity.

The first boatload of stampeders arrived in Skagway Bay on July 26, 1897. Soon ships were disgorging hundreds of

(Right) An early view of Healy's trading post prior to or as the gold rush was beginning. This was the first trading post to be built, not only in Dyea, but all of Alaska.
(Below) The exterior of Healy and Wilson's trading post on Declaration Day, 1899.

(Above) This false front is thought to be the remains of a real estate office built in Dyea in 1898. A photograph taken in the spring of 1898 shows the words A.W. Gregg Real Estate painted on the structure. When photographed in 1988, it was the last standing false-front in Dyea.
(Opposite page) An aerial view of Dyea Flats, and the Dyea Valley, leading to Chilkoot Pass.
(Below) This mural depicting various construction activities along the WP&YR was designed and painted by Charles Baker and Roy Minter.

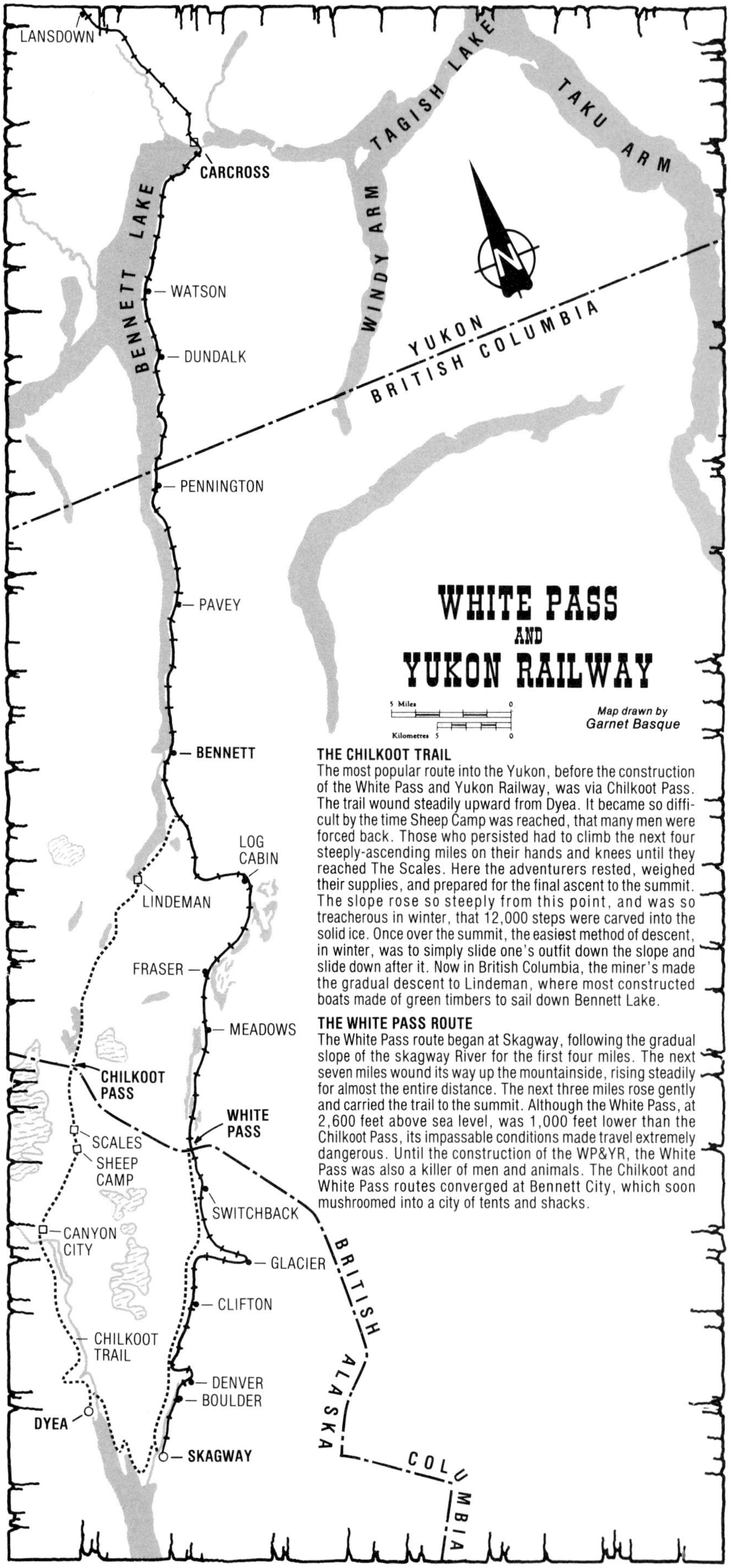

GEORGE BRACKETT

CHARLES WILKENSON

WILLIAM CLOSE

WHITE PASS
AND
YUKON RAILWAY

Map drawn by
Garnet Basque

THE CHILKOOT TRAIL

The most popular route into the Yukon, before the construction of the White Pass and Yukon Railway, was via Chilkoot Pass. The trail wound steadily upward from Dyea. It became so difficult by the time Sheep Camp was reached, that many men were forced back. Those who persisted had to climb the next four steeply-ascending miles on their hands and knees until they reached The Scales. Here the adventurers rested, weighed their supplies, and prepared for the final ascent to the summit. The slope rose so steeply from this point, and was so treacherous in winter, that 12,000 steps were carved into the solid ice. Once over the summit, the easiest method of descent, in winter, was to simply slide one's outfit down the slope and slide down after it. Now in British Columbia, the miner's made the gradual descent to Lindeman, where most constructed boats made of green timbers to sail down Bennett Lake.

THE WHITE PASS ROUTE

The White Pass route began at Skagway, following the gradual slope of the skagway River for the first four miles. The next seven miles wound its way up the mountainside, rising steadily for almost the entire distance. The next three miles rose gently and carried the trail to the summit. Although the White Pass, at 2,600 feet above sea level, was 1,000 feet lower than the Chilkoot Pass, its impassable conditions made travel extremely dangerous. Until the construction of the WP&YR, the White Pass was also a killer of men and animals. The Chilkoot and White Pass routes converged at Bennett City, which soon mushroomed into a city of tents and shacks.

passengers, large quantities of supplies and untold numbers of horses and mules. In the stampede, Moore's land claims were brushed aside, and by mid-August, the population had swelled to the point that a committee was elected to oversee construction of the booming settlement.

Skagway and Dyea developed in much the same way, but Skagway had two distinct advantages over its rival. First, it boasted a deep water harbour where ships could unload right at the wharf. Second, the White Pass was considerably lower than the Chilkoot, and was touted as being the only pass through which horses could easily be driven. In the beginning the White Pass route looked easy, so many prospectors brought pack horses. Higher up, however, the trail wound through a long, narrow ravine. Cluttered with deadfalls, which no one bothered to remove, and huge boulders, many of which had to be climbed over, the route was virtually impassable to horses. Some 3,000 horses were shot or abandoned to die, and this place became known as "Dead Horse Gulch."

NWMP Comm. James Walsh, who visited the White Pass in the autumn of 1897, was greeted by the horrendous sight. Swore Walsh: "Such a scene of havoc and destruction as we encountered can scarcely be imagined. . . . The inhumanity which this trail has been witness to, the heartbreaking which so many have undergone, cannot be imagined."

The first serious threat to Dyea's transportation monopoly came from George Brackett, who, by the fall of 1897, had begun construction on a wagon road up the White Pass. Iron-ically, Brackett had initially viewed the Chilkoot as the most likely route for a wagon road. But others were able to convince Brackett that the White Pass was the transportation route of the future, so he directed his efforts there instead. Meanwhile, a far more serious threat to Dyea's survival, the White Pass & Yukon Railway (WP&YR), was about to make its presence felt.

In 1897, 32 railroad companies applied for federal charters to build lines into the Yukon. That same year 10 were incor-porated in British Columbia, while between 1897 and 1899 another 12 filed articles of incorporation in the United States.

Ironically, the one railroad scheme that finally succeeded was not included in any of the above, and was not a direct result of the Klondike stampede. In December 1895, a group of English capitalist formed a syndicate known as the British Columbia Development Association (BCDA). Two weeks later Charles H. Wilkinson, a member of the syndicate, was en route to B.C. looking for investment opportunities.

In Victoria, Wilkinson was met by Ernest Billinghurst, a brother of another member of the BCDA. Billinghurst lost little time in informing Wilkinson about Captain Moore's scheme to develop a route through the White Pass. After a meeting with Moore, Wilkinson was intrigued enough in the possibility that he sent Billinghurst to Skagway for a first-hand examina-tion.

Billinghurst was impressed by what he saw, although he felt the route was better suited for a wagon road than a railway. Based on his report, a decision was reached in April, 1896, to proceed with some sort of transportation project. The fol-lowing month an agreement was reached with Moore that provided him with the $1,450 needed to complete his wharf and develop his land in Skagway.

A year later, on April 22, 1897, the 30-mile section of railway through the province of British Columbia from White Pass to the Yukon border was incorporated as the British Columbia-Yukon Railway Company. Two months later, on June 29, the section from the Yukon border to Fort Selkirk, its originally proposed destination, was incorporated as the British Yukon Mining, Trading and Transportation Company. The only sec-tion of the charter that remained to be incorporated was the 20-mile section from Skagway to the top of White Pass. Actu-ally, The Pacific and Arctic Railway and Navigation Company had been incorporated in West Virginia prior to the other two sections, but it would be May, 1898, before the right of wav would finally be granted.

In the meantime, however, the BCDA reached the conclusion that they could not financially undertake such a railway pro-ject. Instead, they agreed to transfer all their rights to Wilkin-son. In return, Wilkinson agreed to pay £10,000 on January 9, 1898, and a further £20,000 on May 9. Wilkinson, however, did not have the necessary funds, and he sought anxiously for backers.

Wilkinson eventually was put in contact with William Close, of the English financial firm of Close Brothers & Company. After several meetings, Close Brothers agreed to loan Wilkin-son the £10,000 necessary for the first part of the transaction. The agreement stipulated that if Wilkinson was unable to repay the loan, Close Brothers would have the right to assume the company's assets.

Meanwhile, in February, 1898, a new player entered the game. Michael J. Heney, an unemployed railroad contractor, had been intrigued by the transportation problems posed by the Chilkoot and White passes that he had read so much about in the newspapers. Without financing or backers, Heney de-cided to travel to Skagway and conduct his own survey of the White Pass. In fact, Heney was so financially strapped that he had to borrow money for his passage north.

Once in Skagway, Heney lost little time in evaluating the situation. Although he soon learned about the competition from the three tramways operating from Dyea, Heney realized that the more immediate problem was Brackett's wagon road. Heney travelled the wagon road, already completed to within four miles of White Pass summit, then followed the rough trail to Lake Bennett, studying the formidable character of the terrain and trying to determine the feasibility of a railroad. It did not take him long to realize that such a project would be faced with numerous construction problems and obstacles, not to mention the sub-arctic winters. But as he made his way back to Skagway, he was confident the scheme could succeed if given the proper financing.

Meanwhile, Wilkinson had not been able to repay Close Brothers their £10,000 loan, and it was becoming apparent that he would not be able to raise the remaining £20,000 needed to complete his option purchase. Close Brothers now faced the real possibility of losing their initial investment. To prevent this, Close Brothers paid the remaining £20,000 and took control of the enterprise. Samuel H. Graves, the chief executive officer of Close Brothers' North American operation, was chosen to oversee the project.

Before construction could begin, however, a thorough sur-vey would have to be undertaken. With this goal in mind, Sir. Thomas Tancred left England in March, 1898. In New York Tancred was joined by Erastus C. Hawkins, a civil engineer, and his assistant John Hislop. On April 10, the three men landed in Skagway and registered at the St. James Hotel.

The three men were immediately faced with two major problems. First, Captain Moore had not been able to obtain title to his 160 acres at Skagway, leaving the matter of a right of way very much in question. Second, Brackett's wagon road,

(Above) The summit of Chilkoot Pass, looking into Alaska, 1983.
(Right) An old kitchen range at Canyon City.
(Below) The Chilkoot Trail as it winds its way around Crater Lake.

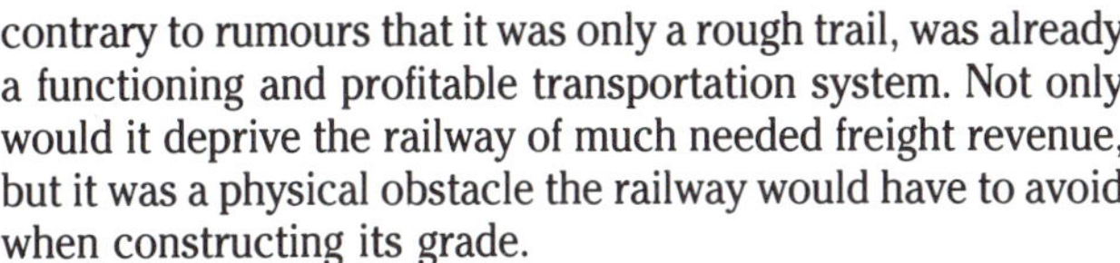

(Above) The remains of the old tramway cable near the top of Chilkoot Pass, June 1983.
(Top left) This 1899 photo of Canyon City shows the tramline carrying goods through the air.
(Left) The remains of boots left by a Klondike stampeder rests at Lindeman City. Like Bennett City a mile further, Lindeman became a city of tents with a migratory population of 10,000.

contrary to rumours that it was only a rough trail, was already a functioning and profitable transportation system. Not only would it deprive the railway of much needed freight revenue, but it was a physical obstacle the railway would have to avoid when constructing its grade.

To counter the first problem, a Skagway bank was instructed to quietly purchase lots along the right of way on behalf of Close Brothers. To counter the second, Hawkins offered to purchase Brackett's entire wagon road operation. But Brackett, who was raking in up to $2,000 a day on toll charges, had no inclination to sell. Instead, he offered to sell the right of way on the lower section for $206,000 — an offer that Hawkins rejected.

As surveys of the proposed railway route were undertaken, new problems began to emerge. Finally, after only one week of surveys, Tancred began to have serious doubts about the feasibility of the entire project. Each night Tancred, Hawkins and Hislop would meet in the lobby of the St. James Hotel, and, over drinks, would discuss the mounting problems well into the early morning. Hawkins and Hislop remained optimistic that the railway could be built, but as the nights passed, it became obvious that Tancred's recommendations to London would be negative. It was beginning to look as if the entire

project was doomed.

One night, when the situation appeared desperate, fate intervened. Tancred, Hawkins and Hislop were about to retire for the night when a weary individual entered the hotel and asked for a room. Upon being informed that Michael Heney was a railway contractor who had just returned from conducting a survey through White Pass to Bennett City, Hawkins invited him over for drinks.

While a sceptical Tancred sat and listened, Heney, Hawkins and Hislop discussed the project well into the night. Finally, Heney's enthusiasm and arguments began to sway Tancred, and by morning he too became convinced in the viability of the project.

In Tancred's favourable report to London he estimated the total cost of construction at $1,570,000. Because the route was so formidable, he advised Close Brothers that construction costs would be at least double the standard for most railways in the United States. Furthermore, upon completion, the cost of maintaining the system would be four times normal.

With the go ahead from Close Brothers, the first problem faced by the company was logistical. Supplies had to be transported from Vancouver, Victoria or Seattle, over 1,000 miles away. This problem was further complicated by the fact that the only means of transporting the supplies to Skagway was by steamer, most of which were already taxed to the limit with stampeders. To overcome the shortage of vessels, the WP&YR accumulated the wrecks and hulks of old ships, patched them up and converted them to freight-carrying barges. These were then towed back and forth with men and equipment.

Next, manpower would have to be found, for thousands of workers would be needed. With gold fever raging throughout the north, the temperament of the majority of men allowed for little enthusiasm to work for wages. But, apart from specialists brought from the south, men were eventually recruited. Most of the workers were men who, through some misfortune, such as losing their money to the nefarious Soapy Smith and his cronies, had little option. They were of all nationalities and status. Many simply wanted to earn enough money to obtain passage home from this god-forsaken land.

A surprising large percentage of the workers were well educated professionals, including doctors and lawyers, who swung picks and shovels for a few dollars a day. Crews worked hard and long, earning $3 per 10-hour day. The quality of the

labour force caused President Graves to comment: "Probably no other railway in the world was built by such highly educated men as worked on the route up the pass."

By April, 1898, enough supplies had arrived to allow some work to be started, although it was essentially small hand work using wheelbarrows, picks and shovels. It was not until May 28, when some steel rails were landed, that construction of the WP&YR officially began. Within 48 hours Heney, who had been hired as general foreman, had over 100 men and horses at work on the outskirts of Skagway.

Once again the problem of right of way surfaced. The railway's eventual route would be along Skagway's east bluff. To ensure access, on May 18 the railway purchased the assets of the financially strapped Skagway and Lake Bennett Tramway Company. Unfortunately, part of the land was occupied by squatters who refused to move. To avoid delays, the railway sought a temporary right of way down Broadway, Skagway's main street.

Skagway's general population, who saw the benefits of the railroad, were mostly in favour. However, the businessmen of Broadway held a different view. They envisioned their bus-

(Right) Heading for the Klondike via Dyea Inlet, Alaska, 1897. Some fortune seekers believed in being fully equipped, such as these optimists who are armed with mattress and rocking chair. But high hopes and good intentions soon fell victim to the realities of the trail. Today, nearly a century after, a veritable junkyard marks the historic Chilkoot Trail, its original travellers having abandoned everything but the proverbial kitchen sink in the need to lighten their loads.
(Below) A street scene in Canyon City with horse-drawn sleigh in front of the Red Onion Hotel and Canyon City Hotel, 1899.

iness being disrupted or destroyed by gangs of construction crews working down the centre of Broadway, and were opposed. This left Skagway's *ad hoc* council caught in the middle. As meeting after meeting followed, some of them heated, the councilmen started leaning toward the desire of the railway and the will of the majority of Skagway's citizens. Finally, on June 14, Supt. Frank Whiting was advised by the town council that a permit would be issued the following morning, after yet another meeting. But Whiting had seen enough delays, and instructed Heney to put the Broadway construction plans into motion during the night. When the citizens of Skagway awoke the following morning, they were surprised to see a force of 200 men ripping up the centre of Broadway. Four days later Heney's men had completed the first mile of railway grade through downtown Skagway.

With the right of way problem now behind them, there remained two major obstacles to the railway's long term viability. Competition from the Chilkoot tramways was a continuing threat and would eventually have to be dealt with, but of more immediate concern was Brackett's wagon·road. As construction of the WP&YR progressed through Skagway, Hawkins tried again to purchase the entire wagon road assets. Brackett, however, was still demanding $206,000, the amount he needed to retire his own debts and still make a profit. Hawkins' rejection meant the railway was forced to make a costly four mile-long detour, spanning the Skagway River twice, to circumvent Brackett's road.

In late June, Brackett and Hawkins met in Seattle to discuss the purchase of the wagon road. Hawkins' repeated attempts had failed to get Brackett to budge, so he wired the railway's president, Samuel Graves, to join them. The bargaining position of both parties had strengths and weaknesses, and each was known to the other side.

For Brackett, he needed money to pay his debts. He also knew that when the railway was completed, his road would be doomed. On the plus side, however, the railway needed the use of his road to transport men, equipment and supplies to their work sites. As for the railway, their work was constantly throwing debris on the wagon road, which required time and effort to clear. They also had to cross the road several times. And, while they knew the railway could eventually kill the wagon road, Brackett threatened to lower his freight rates to prices the railway could never hope to compete with. The solution to everyone's problem was for Brackett to sell his wagon road to the railway. The only obstacle to that solution was the stiff price demanded by Brackett. Neither side appeared willing to budge.

Finally, Brackett made a new proposal. He would give the railway unlimited access to his road for $50,000. He also agreed to dismiss all current and future claims against the railroad arising out of damage caused by blasting and construction. For a further $10,000, Brackett would also give the railway an option to purchase the wagon road outright for an additional $50,000. In the meantime, Brackett would continue to operate the wagon road and collect tolls, and if the railway did not exercise its option by July 1, 1899, the wagon road would remain his. Graves agreed immediately.

Meanwhile, back at Skagway, construction was continuing. On July 20, 1898, a locomotive hauled two flat-cars loaded with construction supplies seven miles to the end of steel, at Rocky Point. The next day the first passenger train ever to operate in Alaska, consisting of the same two flat-cars fitted with rows of benches, left Skagway for the same destination.

Rocky Point, a sheer mountain of granite that rose 800 feet from the valley floor, posed what many predicted to be an insurmountable obstacle. Roy Minter, in his classic book *The White Pass,* described this formidable barrier.

"They first had to establish a construction line that would cross the face of the cliff 700 feet above the floor of the valley. Then they had to blast out a 16-foot-wide shelf to carry the roadbed and track around this massive obstruction. Several engineers who were headed for the Klondike openly ridiculed the builders' boast that they could cut a roadbed across the upper reaches of this seemingly impregnable mass of rock.

"Heney's initial task at Rocky Point was to prepare and detonate a series of blasts, which would clear an approach to the main obstacle, a hugh buttress of rock 120 feet high, 70 feet wide and 20 feet thick — a 20,000-ton granite plug that some had said would stop the railway builders cold. Heney's plan was to honeycomb the obstruction with blast chambers, charge them with black powder, and blow the upper face off the cliff. This, he claimed, would provide him with a narrow ledge, a rough-hewn toehold from which he would mount his final attack, creating a railway roadbed notched in the side of the mountain spur.

"To start the Rocky Point cut, the drillers and rock men were swung down the side of the cliff on ropes, a gymnastic practice that would characterize much of the rock work between Skagway and the summit. After chipping out the narrow ledges on which to stand, they attacked the sheer cliff with drills and two-man and three-man jacks. Gradually they enlarged their footholds and began to develop the blasting plan designed by Hawkins and Heney. . . .

"For days on end, Heney's crews drilled and blasted the cliff, pulverizing the rock with a series of black-powder charges that Heney claimed rivalled the noise of Admiral Dewey's bombardment of Manila. The constant boom of the blasts, the smell of blasting powder, and the swirling clouds of dust irritated the eyes and ears and noses of the packers and gold seekers who toiled along the valley floor. 'Sometimes more than 100,000 tons of granite were dislodged by a single battery blast,' Graves later reported to the company's English shareholders. One charge blasted off a huge slice of rock that fell with a deafening roar into the Skagway River, changing its course. The expense was enormous; powder and dynamite cost more than $600 per ton delivered from Seattle to the site. Rocky Point alone consumed more than 250 tons of explosives, and it was only the first string of obstacles that faced Hawkins and Heney and their inexperienced workers."

Construction from the sea to the summit was extremely difficult and hazardous. Immediately upon leaving Skagway flat the railway became distinctive. It had one of the steepest grades in North America, averaging 3.9 percent, with extremely sharp curves of up to 20 percent.

Nevertheless, through June and July, crews worked in two 10-hour shifts, trying to reach the summit by September. Rocky Point was eventually beaten, and by the first of August, 16 miles of the route had been graded and track had been laid for the first eight.

Then, on August 7, the railway suffered a serious setback. Retaining the workforce in the madness of a major gold rush was one of the greatest problems faced by the WP&YR. Many labourers worked only long enough to get a grubstake before leaving for the Yukon, or returning home. But these problems seemed insignificant on August 7 when three miners stopped at White Pass City and displayed 14 pounds of gold they had

(Above) WP&YR excursion train near the summit of White Pass.
(Opposite page) Spectacular Pitchfork Falls at Milepost 11.5.
(Below) A winter scene at Glacier Station on the WP&YR.

MICHAEL HENEY

ERASTUS HAWKINS

JOHN HISLOP

mined at Atlin. The next day some 800 men were lined up demanding their salary. Many others had not even bothered to wait for their pay, hurrying off to the Atlin goldfields, taking thousands of dollars worth of picks, shovels and other railway equipment with them. Of the over 2,000 men who had been employed, only 700 remained.

Attempts to replace the miners who had left seemed hopeless. Wrote Roy Minter: "Of 250 new recruits, who had arrived in Skagway 10 days after the Atlin stampede, only eight were induced to stay on the job. The rest followed the rush to Atlin."

The railway wanted 2,500 men, but it seemed impossible. As soon as 100 new recruits were hired, 100 more would quit. It was a frustrating situation of massive turnovers, but the railway finally succeeded in increasing the force to 1,200.

Despite the setback, by mid-August, the WP&YR was offering limited service from Skagway to Rocky Point. Later that month, three more locomotives, 10 additional flatcars and three passenger coaches were shipped from Seattle.

As construction costs mounted and delays slowed progress, the goal of reaching the summit by the end of September soon came and went. Between construction crews and the summit stood three major obstacles. The first, Sliding Rock, was a smooth rock face with a 60 degree slope. Just as they had at Rocky Point, men hung suspended by ropes as they cut a narrow foothold for a roadbed. The next obstacle was a mountain, through which a tunnel would have to be blasted. But to get there, crews first had to construct a long wooden trestle over a 150-foot-wide chasm known as Glacier Gorge.

Possibly no other tunnel in the world was constructed with greater difficulty than this one. Although only 250 feet long, the tunnel had to penetrate a perpendicular barrier of rock jutting out high up a mountainside. Machinery and equipment for the task had to be lifted by hand up the vertical face that offered the barest of footholds. Once again, the men had to be attached by ropes for safety. Then, as the tunnel progressed during the winter, doors had to be placed on the portals to keep snow from blocking the passage and the freezing rain from blasting through. It was January 29, 1899, before the tunnel was finally completed through the mountain.

Three miles further, at Mile 19 from Skagway, the infamous Dead Horse Gulch blocked the railroad. No ordinary trestle would span the 1,200-foot gorge, and it would take months to erect a metal cantilever bridge. To avoid delay, service was provided by a switchback. (In 1901, a spectacular cantilever bridge was erected to replace the switchback. When completed it was not only the most northerly, but, at 215 feet, also the highest railway bridge in the world.)

Construction of the WP&YR to this point had been difficult and dangerous, but at least the weather had not made conditions even more hazardous. Now, as the weeks wore on, men were often stopped dead in their tracks by intense cold, vicious blizzards, immense snowdrifts, and relentless, howling winds. It is almost unbelievable that the men were able to work during the full fury of that extremely cold sub-arctic winter. This ultra-severe cold made the workers torpid and benumbed in both mind and body. After one hour's work it was often necessary to relieve the men with a fresh crew.

The extreme cold created other problems as well. It froze switches which could only be kept open by a steady fire. It made the rails so icy that, when going uphill, the locomotive wheels would spin despite the use of sand. And, to keep the locomotives running, special crews were needed to keep torches applied to the oil cups.

Very deep snowfalls were another difficulty. Between Skagway and Bennett the snow varied between eight and 12 feet, but the worse snows were between the summit and Log Cabin. When the snow was more than 12 feet deep, which it often was, especially in slides, the rotary snowploughs could not clear the rails until the snow above the 12-foot level had been removed by hand shovel. On occasions the passengers had to come to the assistance of the crew in this task.

The sub-arctic shortness of daylight hours created yet another problem. The sun would rise at nine or 10 in the morning and set between two and four in the afternoon. But even these shortened hours were impaired by the low clouds around the summit that often befogged the area.

Meanwhile, the three Chilkoot aerial tramways had been merged as the Chilkoot Railway & Transport Company. They now offered a total freight service from Dyea, over the summit of Chilkoot Pass to Crater Lake by a system of freight wagons and tramways. From there a packer service connected to Lake Lindeman and Bennett City. Wallace, the company's president,

Broadway Street, Skagway in 1898, showing construction workers constructing the grade.

then issued circulars to southern shippers extolling the virtues of his Chilkoot Pass tramway and his company's ability to handle any amount of freight. With rates that were less than the railway, it remained a serious threat.

Not to be outdone, the railway placed its own ads in west coast newspapers. In addition, both companies had agents in ports along the coast trying to divert freight to their own enterprise. With both sides embellishing the truth, freight forwarders did not know who or what to believe.

The railway's share of freight business, now being offered from Skagway to Heney Station, was increasing weekly. During the same period, Brackett's wagon road was also doing a brisk business. On November 9, 1898, the WP&YR eliminated this competitor by exercising its option. Brackett would be paid $5 for each ton transported over the WP&YR until the full $50,000 was paid.

On February 18, 1899, almost a full year after construction began, the railway crews finally reached the 2,885-foot summit of White Pass. Over its 20-mile course were 37 bridges, with a combined length of 4,095 feet, and 2,685 feet of snowsheds.

From White Pass, freight was transported over a sleigh road

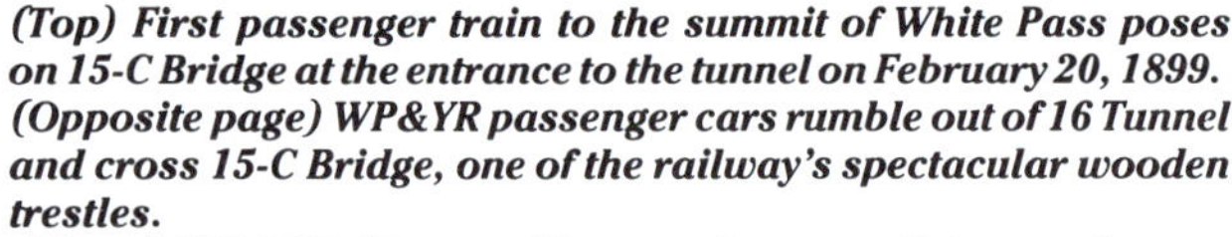

*(Top) First passenger train to the summit of White Pass poses on 15-C Bridge at the entrance to the tunnel on February 20, 1899.
(Opposite page) WP&YR passenger cars rumble out of 16 Tunnel and cross 15-C Bridge, one of the railway's spectacular wooden trestles.
(Above) WP&YR "Bennett Motorcar" uses a Fairmont "power car," a baggage car, and a passenger trailer.
(Right) WP&YR excursion train near summit at Mile 19.3.
(Below) Old Lake Bennett depot (now closed) still greets hikers and day passengers for twice daily departures of the WP&YR rail/motorcar service.*

LAKE KLUKSHU
LAKE McCLINTOCK
LAKE KUSAWA

Railroad construction crews hacking out the right-of-way using picks, shovels and black powder at Rocky Point. This is the deep, narrow canyon of the Skagway River near Mile 7 on the WP&YR in the summer of 1898.

to Log Cabin station, which served as headquarters for the NWMP and Canada Customs. From Log Cabin, which, at an elevation of 2,916 feet was the highest point of the rails, the trail sloped downhill until it reached Bennett Lake at Mile 41. To facilitate the delivery from the summit to Log Cabin or Bennett, the WP&YR formed the Red Line Transportation Company, although its sleighs were unable to keep pace with the enormous tonnage of freight being disgorged by the railway.

By this time the WP&YR had 1,800 construction workers on the payroll. For reasons already stated, it had always been difficult to retain workers. To entice them to stay, the work day had previously been shortened to nine hours and the wages had been increased to 35¢ an hour. But in late April the railway rolled back the wages to 30¢ an hour. The men refused to accept a pay cut and by March 2 more than 1,200 were on strike. Skagway supported the railway's position, while Dyea's businessmen, realizing that a strike-bound railway would divert thousands of tons of freight and much business to Dyea, threw their support behind the strikers.

For a brief period the Dyea tramways appeared to gain the upper hand. Their advertisements had been so successful that the tramline was receiving more freight business than it could handle. In addition to that, their agents were snatching freight from under the noses of the railway on the Skagway wharves.

When the strike ended on March 17, however, the future of the tramways appeared gloomy. In response, Wallace announced plans to extend his tramway service from Crater Lake to Bennett, at a cost of $300,000. Because construction costs for the railway were so much higher, Wallace was confident the tramway could compete successfully with the railway.

Other directors of the tramway were not so sure. They were afraid that when the railway was completed to Bennett their tramways would become obsolete and they would lose their entire investment. So when the railway offered to buy them out in May for $100,000, they accepted. By this time railway construction crews had completed all rock work between Fraser Lake and Bennett. As the weather improved, and the tempo of construction increased, Hawkins predicted the railway would reach Bennett by July 1. Later the weather made him revise that estimate to sometime between July 12 and July 15.

To meet the self-imposed deadline, 871 men were spread out along the route, and by mid-June a rough grade had been completed to Bennett. On June 21, men started laying rails from the summit, and by the following day, over three miles had been laid down. By June 28, the tracks were more than eight miles into British Columbia, and by July 1, the rails had been pushed passed Log Cabin. Two days later it was within three miles of Bennett, where construction was temporarily delayed because of an unfinished bridge. Working all night, the bridge gang completed the bridge by the following morning. By noon tracks had been laid across the deck and work trains passed through. Two days later, on July 6, 1899, the WP&YR reached Bennett. One week later Hawkins closed down the Chilkoot tramways and dismantled the equipment. The WP&YR had eliminated all competitors and now enjoyed an undisputed monopoly on all freight moving into Bennett, or so it thought.

On October 12, a firm calling itself the Dyea and Chilkoot Railway Company announced plans to begin construction of a railway from Dyea to Whitehorse via the Chilkoot Pass. In a copy of the Notice which appeared in the Bennett *Sun,* the company made an application "to construct, equip, operate and maintain a railway from a point on or near the Dyea river on the International Boundary between British Columbia and Alaska to a point at or near Lake Bennett, thence to the 60th parallel of latitude, with power to equip, construct and operate branch lines; to build, own and maintain docks and wharves, own and operate telegraph and telephone lines; to generate electric power for lighting and heating; to expropriate land necessary for the said railway; to levy and collect tolls and to make traffic arrangements incidental to said line of railway."

Included in the project was a proposal to drive a tunnel, which NWMP Superintendent Wood reported was to be 12 feet high, 10 feet wide and 3,800 feet long, beneath Chilkoot Pass summit. Commenting on the scheme, the *Daily Alaskan* reported that "should the Chilkoot tunnel be pushed to completion and the proposed railroad be built over the pass from Dyea, the line thus created would prove a lusty rival to the WP&YR, forcing it to act on the defensive, as it did in the case of the Chilkoot tramlines — and buy out the impending rival."

Local newspapers reported that 11 men were already at work on the tunnel, which would cost $250,000 to build, and mules and manpower were already on the scene. C.H. DeWitt, a general contractor, had been awarded a $45,000 contract to construct a railway grade to the mouth of the proposed tunnel.

Despite the publicity and hoopla, however, very little was ever accomplished. DeWitt was never paid, so he pulled his outfit out of Dyea and went to Bennett City.

Meanwhile, although the railway was completed from Skagway to Bennett Lake on July 6, 1899, it would be another year before the tracks being laid southward from Whitehorse would connect up.

Hugging the eastern shore of Bennett Lake, the line would establish stations at Pavey and Pennington, the latter just below the Yukon border. Once into the Yukon, the line passed two more stations, Dundalk and Watson, before arriving at Caribou Crossing (Carcross), so named because it offered a natural ford for animals. Until the railroad was connected, service from Carcross and Whitehorse was provided by sternwheelers, in summer, and horse-drawn wagons or sleighs in winter.

After 27 months of valiant effort, the north and south sections of the WP&YR met at Carcross on July 29, 1900. The golden spike ceremony was attended by the railroad's first president, Samuel Graves, and numerous Canadian and American dignitaries.

However, because of the lavish Yukon hospitality, the driving of the last spike became more than an historic occasion. After an experienced track man had positioned the golden spike, spectators watched as a senior American official stumbled forward. Selected to "strike the first blow," he completely missed the target. Hislop tried next, but enjoyed no better success. Next came another inebriated official, who, seeing two spikes, struck one a glancing blow that bent it. President Graves was next to take up the challenge and, spurred on by the cheering crowd, finally connected. Later, when no one was around, the track superintendent withdrew the badly damaged spike so workers could replace it. The line completed, regular scheduled service between Skagway and Whitehorse began August 15, 1900. Thirty-five men had been killed during its construction.

PADDLE WHEELS ON THE YUKON RIVER

From Klondike gold rush days through the 1900s, steam-driven stern-wheelers were the main means of transportation on Yukon waterways. Their supremacy ended only with the construction of a highway system linking Whitehorse with Dawson City and other points north.

BETWEEN 1869 and 1937, some 250 steam-driven paddle wheel boats were constructed to ply the Yukon River and other Yukon waterways. Alas, of this vast flotilla, only two have survived to be preserved as National Historic Sites. Maintained by Parks Canada, these are the steamers *Klondike* at Whitehorse, and the *Keno* at Dawson City. Until 1990 there was a third, the *Tutshi* at Carcross, but it was destroyed by fire that summer.

The honour of being the first steamboat on the Yukon River, according to LeRoy "Jack" McQuesten, goes to the *Yukon*. Owned by the Alaska Commercial Company (ACC), the *Yukon* was providing service from St. Michael, an island just off the Alaska coast at the mouth of the Yukon River, to Fort Yukon, as early as 1869. This steamer was so small, wrote McQuesten, "that she had to tow all her goods in barges and she had only accommodation for the crew to handle her. She had no cabin; the stove was in the fire room and four could sit down to the table at a time. The traders in the lower river had to go in the barges and at meal times we would stop and let them come aboard for their meals."

In 1878 a second steamer, the *St. Michael,* owned by the Western Fur and Trading Company, made its appearance. However, when this company failed a short time later, the *St. Michael* was acquired by the ACC. About the same time, the *Yukon,* which had been laid up for the winter at Fort Yukon, was crushed by ice and sank. Fortunately, a replacement for the aging steamer had already been ordered. The frame work had been built in San Francisco, then disassembled and shipped to St. Michael. There, three carpenters and all the traders pitched in to build the new steamer. It was launched in four weeks and on August 20 the 75-foot-long *Yukon,* christened

(Above) The stern-wheeler Casca *in the Yukon River before being beached at Whitehorse.*

(Left) The New Racket, *one of the earliest steamers to travel the Yukon River.*

(Right) The first steamer to visit Dawson. Although no year is specified, judging by the undeveloped nature of the waterfront, this photo was probably taken in 1897 or 1898.

in honour of the original, left St. Michael.

In 1882, a small steamer called the *New Racket,* which had been shipped from San Francisco on the deck of a schooner, made its appearance. A short time later it was acquired by the ACC. In 1889, to keep pace with the burgeoning demand for goods and services, the ACC built the *Arctic,* a powerful boat nearly twice the length of any steamer then operating on the Yukon River. Later that year she made her maiden voyage to the new gold rush town of Fortymile, which already boasted 10 saloons. In 1892 the North American Trading & Transportation Company added the *Porteous B. Weare* to the small fleet of stern-wheelers already operating on the Yukon, followed, in 1895, by the ACC's 400-ton *Alice* at St. Michael.

All of these early stern-wheelers were providing service on the Yukon River, generally from St. Michael to Fortymile, prior to the Klondike gold rush. Although the major discoveries of Bonanza and Eldorado creeks had yet to be made, each year saw an ever-increasing number of miners and entrepreneurs enter the Yukon Valley. Most were centred around the towns of Circle City, in Alaska, and Fortymile, in the Yukon, and their surrounding, gold-laden creeks. George Carmack's discovery on August 17, 1896, changed all that.

The *Arctic,* which reached Fortymile shortly after the news of the Bonanza Creek discovery, pushed upriver through ice flows to the mouth of the Klondike. She arrived in September with a few miners and a very limited amount of freight, being the first steamer to visit Dawson City, the new town then in its very infancy. After discharging men and freight, the *Arctic* hurried back to Fortymile, but was frozen in before she could be placed in a safe location. Next spring, in trying to get her free of the ice before she was crushed, a stick of dynamite intended for the ice destroyed her.

In July, 1897, following the arrivals of the *Excelsior* and *Portland* in San Francisco and Seattle, thousands of adventurers began a mad dash for the Klondike goldfields. As the migration increased in volume, it created a great demand for river boats. In California, the Pacific Northwest, British Columbia, Alaska and the Yukon, stern-wheelers began to be constructed in unprecedented numbers.

Of the 250 steamers that were eventually constructed for Yukon waterways, information is available on about 150, although much of that is sketchy. Of the 150 that are known about, 25 were built at St. Michael. Of these, the 370-ton *Bella,* built in 1896. was the second steamer to visit Dawson, arriving there in July, 1897. The 134-ton *May West,* built at St. Michael in 1898, was the first steamer to reached Dawson that year, arriving on June 8. Three days later the 55-ton *Victoria,* built in 1897, became the second steamer to reach Dawson that year. Other steamers constructed at St. Michael in 1897 include the 595-ton *Charles H. Hamilton* and the *Margaret.* During 1898, the following steamers were built at St. Michael: *Dusty Diamond,* 101 tons; *Florence S,* 90 tons; *John J. Healy,* 450 tons; *Leah,* 477 tons; *Los Angeles,* 90 tons; *North Star,* 28 tons; the *Seattle* and the *Gold Star.*

Another busy steamer construction site was located at Lake Bennett, in the northwestern tip of British Columbia. Here, in the late fall and winter of 1897, some 10,000 prospectors and entrepreneurs were stalled in their golden quest by winter. As they waited for the ice to break-up, many spent their time constructing boats that would transport them, via lake and river, to the goldfields. On May 29, 1898, the lake became clear of ice and an enormous flotilla of vessels got underway. From a hill behind his office, Supt. Sam Steele of the North West Mounted Police counted over 800 boats under sail on Bennett Lake. "Strange and motley were the craft," he wrote; "Large scows with oxen, cows, horses and dogs on board, well-built skiffs, clumsy, oblong tubs, little better than ordinary boxes; light and serviceable Peterboro' canoes."

But this ragtag flotilla was not the only boats under construction at Bennett City; stern-wheelers were also being built with a vengeance. During the summer, a fleet of small steamers, the largest 90 feet in length, was constructed at Lake Bennett for navigating the rivers and lakes to Dawson. The first of these to steam all the way from Bennett, successfully running through Miles Canyon and the White Horse Rapids, was the *Bellingham.*

Owned by "Messrs. Dingman, Stringer and Wilcox" of Washington, the *Bellingham* was actually constructed in Bellingham Bay in 1897. She was then freighted to Skagway on the deck of the bark *Theobald,* and in a knock-down shape was transported over White Pass to Bennett City at a cost of $2,000. Reassembled, the diminutive steamer, 35 feet long and eight feet wide, puffed to the wharf at Dawson at 4:30 p.m. on June 13. She had started from Bennett with 32 sacks of mail, eight of which were distributed along the route, and 18 passengers.

However, while the *Bellingham* can claim the distinction of being the first steamer to reach Dawson from Bennett *after* the Bonanza Creek discovery, it was not the first to accomplish this feat. That honour goes to the *Witch Hazel,* an even smaller vessel only 27 feet long and six wide, that performed the feat in 1895. Like the *Bellingham,* the *Witch Hazel* was built elsewhere. It was owned by Frank Atkins and E.L. Busnell of Portland, Oregon. In the spring of 1895 it was transported over the Chilkoot Pass by block and tackle. By the time the *Bellingham* reached Dawson, the *Witch Hazel* was a hulk at Fort Cudahy, near Fortymile.

A few days after the *Bellingham* reached Dawson, eight more steamers completed the run, while two others, the *Kalamazoo* and *Joseph Clossett,* were wrecked in the attempt. One of the successful steamers was the 15-ton *A.J. Goddard.* Built in San Francisco but assembled at Lake Bennett, she reached Dawson eight days after the *Bellingham.*

One of the problems facing steamers built at Bennett was Miles Canyon and its treacherous rapids. Once a boat ventured through the rapids, the current was too powerful to permit it to return upstream. Thus, some steamers were built originally for the run from Bennett City to Canyon City, at the head of Miles Canyon. From there, a wooden-railed tramway system, operated by horses, transferred cargo and passengers around the dangerous rapids to Whitehorse. From Whitehorse, steamers who had navigated below Miles Canyon would transport passengers and freight the remainder of the way to Dawson.

The *Clifford Sifton,* built in 1898 for a syndicate of Kansas women, operated on the Whitehorse-Dawson run. Some of the other steamers on this run included the *Iowa, Linderman, Willie Irving* and others. That same year the Bennett Lake and Klondyke Navigation Company constructed three similar steamers at Lake Bennett; the *Flora,* 63 tons; the *Nora,* 67 tons; and the *Ora,* 69 tons. Each were 80 feet long by 16 wide. The *Flora* and *Nora* delivered freight and passengers from Bennett to Canyon City; while the *Ora* operated the Whitehorse-Dawson run.

With the completion of the White Pass & Yukon Railway (WP&YR) to Whitehorse, which diminished the importance of Bennett City and led to the abandoning of Canyon City,

(Top) *The stern-wheeler* A.J. Goddard *towing five barges leaving Bennett, September 1899.*
(Above) *The* Clifford Sifton, Gleaner *and* Australian *docked at Bennett. Note the herd of cattle by the freight shed.*
(Below) *Three stern-wheelers, the* Clifford Sifton, Bailey *and the* Gleaner *docked by a freight shed at Bennett City. A WP&YR locomotive and car in foreground. 1899.*

(Above) The Tutshi *at Carcross in the summer of 1988.*
(Right) *Exterior view of the* Klondike *at Whitehorse.*
(Opposite page) *View of the entrance to Miles Canyon in 1988. During the Klondike stampede most miners walked along the shore while their freight was transported on the Canyon City tramway. (Inset) Today the MV Schwatka takes tourists on excursions through a greatly tamed Miles Canyon.*
(Below) *At the time this photo was taken in 1988, the* Tarahne *was undergoing a stabilization project. It is beached at Atlin, B.C.*

most steamers moved through the rapids for the lower river. The new railway unloaded its tons of freight at Whitehorse, where numerous steamers competed for the business of moving it to Dawson. This fierce rivalry led to price undercutting, which translated into poor service and a general decline in vessel maintenance and safety.

Finally, in 1901, the WP&YR decided to provide its own steamer service from Whitehorse to Dawson and purchased four river boats belonging to the Canadian Development Company. All four stern-wheelers, the 716-ton *Canadian,* the 205-ton *Columbian,* the 654-ton *Sybil*, and the 781-ton *Yukoner,* had been built in Victoria in 1898. The WP&YR also operated a large shipyard in Whitehorse where it constructed its own boats. Whitehorse then became the main centre on the upper river.

St. Michael, where at least 25 steamers are known to have been built, was the busiest shipyard. Seattle, with 19, ranked second, followed by Whitehorse with 17, Bennett City with 13, Unalaska with 10, Victoria with seven, Ballard with six, and Fairbanks with five. The remainder were constructed at various shipyards in California, Washington, British Columbia, Alaska and the Yukon.

The final years of the river boat era (1941-1955) saw only the stern-wheelers *Whitehorse, Keno, Nasutlin, Aksala, Casca,* and *Klondike* on the Yukon River and its tributaries and the passenger steamer *Tutshi* on Tagish Lake and minor waters. By then, all other steamers had met their end through shipwreck or neglect. For many years the decaying hulks of the *Bonanza King,* built in the Aleutians in 1898, and the famous

Yukoner, which made her last trip in 1903, lay in the Whitehorse shipyards. The *Yukoner* was finally sold for fire wood in 1957. The *Aksala* was disassembled in the 1970s and her paddle wheel placed at Mile 913 of the Alaska Highway, just outside of Whitehorse, a sad relic of her glory days.

The *Keno* was built in Whitehorse in 1922 primarily for the 180-mile run upriver from Stewart City, at the Junction of the Yukon and Stewart rivers, to pick up silver-lead concentrate from the Mayo mines. In 1937 the *Keno* was lengthened from 130 feet to 140 feet. At the same time the *Nasutlin* was overhauled and a new *Klondike* and *Casca* built to replace the vessels lost on the Thirtymile River the previous year. These were the last major stern-wheeler building projects in North America.

The *Keno* was the last stern-wheeler to make the 460-mile trip from Whitehorse downstream to Dawson City. Specially refitted for her final run, she carried guests and reporters for radio's "Roving Reporter" series. The voyage lasted from August 29 to September 2, 1960, and daily reports were sent back on this historic final run. The *Keno* is now a museum at Dawson City. For some reason, the *Keno* and *Klondike II* were chosen over the *Whitehorse* to be preserved for future generations as a reminder of Klondike gold rush days. The steamers *Whitehorse* and *Casca* met tragic ends through neglect and a final act of carelessness when they were burned on June 20, 1974. The *Casca,* third of that name, was the flagship of the British Yukon Navigation Company. But the real loss was the historic *Whitehorse.*

Today visitors can wander at leisure through the two re-

Panoramic view of tents and cabins clustered along the banks at Canyon City, at the entrance to Miles Canyon. Three stern-wheelers, W. Ogilvie. **Australian** *and* **Nora** *are docked in foreground. Tramway tracks are visible on shore behind last steamer.*

maining steamers at their final resting places and try to imagine what life must have been like on the river boats in bygone years. But while tourists may thrill to the tales of the Gold Rush of '98, and even imagine for a moment that they are on the deck of a steamer heading for Dawson City, the two silent steamers cannot really begin to convey the atmosphere of life on the old stern-wheelers in their heyday. For those of us who remember the foaming spray from the churning paddle wheels, the burning of the *Whitehorse* and *Casca* was indeed a sad event.

In the summer of 1951 I signed on the steamer *Tutshi* at Carcross. Just south of Whitehorse, Carcross is located on Nares Lake, a small body of water about three miles long, which connects Lake Bennett with Tagish Lake. It was through Carcross, "the Place where the Cariboo Cross," that the Klondike gold seekers passed on their way to Marsh Lake en route to the goldfields. The *Tutshi,* an Indian word meaning deep water, was built at Carcross in 1917 by the British Yukon Navigation Company.

The 167-foot *Tutshi* was originally designed to carry 80 passengers. Later this was increased to 120 berths. I was a galley hand, and one of my jobs was to load food supplies from the Carcross docks. Hundred pound sacks of flour, cases of tinned foods, and other supplies for the galley all had to be loaded by hand.

Although the *Tutshi* had a registered tonnage of 746, she was specifically designed to serve the tourist trade. Her main source of business was the passengers who sailed from Vancouver to Skagway on the coastal liner *Princess Louise.* During a 36-hour stopover at Skagway, many passengers from the *Princess Louise* would ride the WP&YR to Carcross. Here they boarded the *Tutshi* for a 160-mile round trip excursion to some of the most remote regions in northern B.C.

Passengers boarded the vessel about noon, and shortly after the *Tutshi* began its swing through the narrow passage of Nares Lake into the larger bodies of water beyond. The steamer followed a northeasterly route through Tagish Lake, then southward into Taku Arm, a long funnel-shaped corridor bounded by towering mountains which rise straight up out of the dark water. Ben-My-Chree, our destination, lay at the

(Above) "Closeleigh" the original town-site of Whitehorse, was located at the end of the tramline, on the opposite side of the river from present-day Whitehorse. Loaded horse-drawn tramline cars, tents, stern-wheeler Columbia *and log telegraph station, which opened on July 29, 1899 are all visible. (1899)*
(Below) Whitehorse in 1913 with six stern-wheelers docked along the Yukon River.

(Above) **The** Tutshi *photographed from across the Nares River at Carcross in 1988.*
(Below) **The** Tutshi *engulfed in flames on July 25, 1990. Although arson is suspected, no one has ever been charged.*

(Above) The Klondike II *heading upriver from Whitehorse docks in preparation for a u-turn in midstream to bring her in line with the downstream current heading toward Dawson City, summer 1951. This manoeuvre was necessitated by the force of the current and the size of the steamer.*
(Below) Stern-wheelers in drydock at the Whitehorse shipyards, c1949.

head of Taku Arm where the funnel narrows to a point. Here the alluvial plain brought down by the surrounding mountains supported a variety of flowers not seen elsewhere in the sand or gravel soil of the Yukon. Into this garden paradise the passengers disembarked and were greeted by the host of the homestead and served the specialty of the place, dandelion wine. After a brief visit and a view of Taku Glacier in the far distance, the passengers boarded the *Tutshi* and we headed back toward Carcross. Before the service was discontinued in 1936, passengers were also able to disembark at Taku Landing, where they rode a two-and-a-half-mile narrow-gauge railway to Scotia Bay on Atlin Lake. There they boarded the MV *Tarahne,* which ferried them across Atlin Lake to Atlin.

The *Tutshi* sailed from June 1 to October 31 each year, carrying an average of 4,600 passengers a season. However, when the *Princess Louise* changed its schedule in 1955 to only a 12-hour stopover in Skagway, the *Tutshi* was withdrawn from service.

While the *Tutshi* operated, various historic sites were pointed out to the tourist, such as the abandoned Norgold and Engineer mines. But for the crew, the trip meant work, although we too had opportunities to enjoy the voyage during off-duty moments.

That summer we had a cook with us who had a reputation up and down the coast for serving steaming hot meals to the passengers. Unfortunately, the cook was so fanatical about serving hot meals that he kept the galley unbearably hot. All dishes had to be washed by hand, and as we bent over huge steaming sinks full of dirty dishes, the condensation from the steam rolled off the ceiling and dripped on us, adding to the discomfort. No amount of pleading could dissuade the cook from keeping the galley as hot as the meals that come out of it. Thus, while the passengers ate well indeed, they never knew what misery it caused the crew.

During off-duty hours we would gather in the boiler room below decks or in the crew's quarters. A favourite pastime was pilfering the odd tin of special desserts from the overloaded food locker, treats which seemed to find their way to the passengers or the captain's table rather than to the crew. The method followed was this: one of the galley hands would write off the desired item on the inventory and remove it from the pantry. Meanwhile, another crew member would cautiously edge out along the paddle-arm at the stern and wait for the galley hand on the upper deck to drop the tins to him. Then we would all proceed to the privacy of the crew's quarters where we enjoyed our acquisition with great relish. These depredations on the larder, while an infraction of the rules, cost the company little and were sometimes enforced on the crewmen who worked above deck. Consequently, we were somewhat fearful of crossing the deck hands, who had their own rough code of behaviour.

In 1951 my career on the *Tutshi* came to an abrupt end when I was falsely accused of throwing a dozen teapots overboard. Why I or anyone else would have done such a silly thing I never could quite figure out, unless it was a prank played by the deck hands to get the galley hands in trouble.

For 16 years after its retirement, the *Tutshi* was beached at Carcross and left to rot. Finally, in 1971, her weathering remains were purchased by the Yukon government, which intended to restore her. However, it was 1982 before the restorations began in earnest, and the summer of 1988 before she was finally reopened to the public. Although there was nothing to view inside but a shell, some 5,800 visitors toured the vessel

that year. In 1989 some 10,000 visitors toured the stern-wheeler, and the figures for the first half of 1990 indicated that number would have doubled. But, On July 25, disaster struck.

It was about 12:25 a.m. when flames were detected on the historic steamer. According to Stewart Breithaupt, an Anglican minister who lives in a log cabin a few hundred yards from the vessel, the fire appeared to have originated at the rear near the stern-wheel. Although the fire had only been going about 15 minutes when first detected, it quickly spread to the upper decks and raced through the vessel to the bow.

Volunteer fire-fighters were on the scene quickly. From 12:30 to 2:30 they valiantly fought the blaze with a fire truck and water pumped from a station on the WP&YR bridge. But their efforts proved to be useless. According to the Whitehorse *Star:* "Flames rose up to 175 feet above the boat, threatening to spread into the town of 342 people."

Fortunately for Carcross, known for its notoriously high winds, the air was relatively calm during the fire, although RCMP Const. Pat Egan told a *Star* reporter: "Big cinder chips were blowing right at the Caribou Hotel at one point during a high wind."

The Yukon government had spent about $1,000,000 renovating the *Tutshi,* but had not yet installed a sprinkler system. As for the fire itself, arson is suspected. According to a Whitehorse *Star* article dated August 17, a "Molotov cocktail was found beside the S.S. *Tutshi* by an employee just one week before the tragic fire. . . ." The employee, Jim Borisenko, found "a bottle filled with gas with a rag wick" and turned it over to the local detachment of the RCMP, who, according to the report, "didn't take it seriously."

On November 9, 1990, the Skagway *News* reported the following item: "WHITEHORSE — The Yukon Fire Marshall's office and the RCMP have been unable to determine the cause of the fire that destroyed the historic S.S. *Tutshi* and visitor reception center on July 25 in Carcross.

"According to an Oct. 26 press release from the Yukon Government, the RCMP investigation is continuing and both agencies will continue to follow up on any new leads that come to their attention.

"'Because the fire was so severe, we were unable to uncover any physical evidence indicating the cause,' (Fire Prevention Officer) Johnson said. 'The interviews with people on the scene produced conflicting information, so no firm conclusions as to the cause of the fire could be made by their statements.'

"An RCMP investigation into a report a 'Molotov Cocktail' had been found on the *Tutshi* several weeks before the fire concluded that the one-litre plastic oil container of mixed gasoline 'was used simply to store the liquid and did not have the characteristics of an incendiary device,' according to the press release."

After my dismissal from the *Tutshi* in 1951, I returned to Whitehorse where I was soon exonerated by the White Pass and Yukon Route Shipping Company. I was then reassigned to the steamer *Whitehorse* for the 460-mile run from Whitehorse to Dawson City.

Built in 1901 on the very same spot where she finally burned, the *Whitehorse* was nicknamed "the Old Grey Mare." She was 181 feet long, 36 feet wide, five feet deep, and registered to carry 764 tons. With 46 passenger rooms she could, if required, accommodate 92 passengers. The *Whitehorse* was one of the last real working paddle-wheelers on the Yukon River. In 1951

(Above) The stern-wheeler Keno *at Dawson in the summer of 1988.*
(Below) The Casca *and* Whitehorse *ablaze in 1974. Grown men actually cried as these historic steamers, last of a fleet of 250, burned to the ground despite valiant attempts to save them. The fire was set by transients.*

she was still in full operation as a cargo vessel. In 1954 she made 13 round trips from Whitehorse to Dawson City. The thirteenth trip proved unlucky for "the Old Grey Mare" however, and she was permanently beached and left to rot.

I signed on the *Whitehorse* as a galley hand on July 14, 1951, and we began the run to Dawson City. Because of the steamer's size, and the force of the current, the pilot first had to head upriver from the Whitehorse docks towards Whitehorse Rapids. Then, after making a U-turn in midstream in order to bring the steamer into position, we began the down river run to Dawson. The trip down river took about a day and a half, including a stop for wood. The return trip, against a current of some six knots, with half a dozen stops for wood, usually took four or five days. Major stops for the *Whitehorse* included Carmack, Minto, and the mouth of the Stewart River. Today the riverside communities of Hootalinqua, Big Salmon, Little Salmon, Yukon Crossing, Minto, and Fort Selkirk are abandoned and derelict. But in 1951 the river was still bustling with activity.

The Klondike lost much of its romance with the decay of the riverside boat stops. Minto, for example, had an infamous history. For many years it was a river boat stop and site of a roadhouse on the stage route between Whitehorse and Dawson. In 1898 a triple murder took place there over some stolen gold. It was finally abandoned by the natives in 1954 after a series of unsolved murders. In 1971 it was reported that many of the old buildings were still standing, but by 1980 the place had been almost totally destroyed by transients. Only a single log structure remains on the site today.

My main job on the *Whitehorse,* apart from caring for the needs of any special guests the captain might have had on board, was to serve the crew. As on the *Tutshi,* I worked in the galley washing dishes, making coffee for the crew, and taking care of the food stores. Sometimes I was required to go below decks on some errand for the cook. This could be risky, because the deck hands had the custom of "blackballing" new recruits, especially galley hands. On one occasion when we were tied up at a wood-stop, I was force to crawl out on the narrow outer catwalk which surrounded the lower deck of the *Whitehorse,* while the deck hands tried to corner me between the two side doors. Unable to find anything else at hand, they had decided to use mustard on me. Fortunately, we were close enough to the river-bank and I was able to leap to safety, and thereby escape that initiation at least. Needless to say, however, I did not venture below decks any more than was absolutely necessary.

At these wood-stops along the river-bank the deck hands loaded on board the four-foot cordwood needed to fuel the boilers. A ramp was run from the embankment behind the loaded wood-carts. Sometimes a deck hand would miss the 90-degree turn at the entrance to the engine-room and run the cart off into the river on the other side of the boat. During one loading I made the mistake of commenting to one of the Indian hands, a rather slim, weak-looking lad, that it did not look to be all that hard a job. Without a word he reached over, picked me up as if I had been a rag doll, and set me squarely on the ship's railing. I never again suggested that the deck hands were weaklings. In general there was a fairly good relationship among the crew members and, although we had some very rough characters aboard, I do not recall that any fights ever broke out. Everyone was generally too busy.

Modern travellers on the Yukon River have expressed some disappointment at the relative lack of white water in the famous Five Finger Rapids, just a short distance below Carmacks. Here rock palisades or "flower pot islands" jut out of the river and form a number of channels.

Although it may appear calm today, it was a different matter when the paddle wheel pilot had to manoeuvre his bulky steamer through the right-hand channel on the down river run. The first indication of danger was a sheet of smooth, sharply sloping water, just before the entrance to the narrow channel. Then the huge jutting rock on the left side would flash by so close that you felt you could almost reach out and touch it. Coming back upriver the current was so strong that boats had to be winched through what then became the left-hand channel. To accomplish this, a steel cable was permanently attached to the shore and left to float free in the current, the force of which kept the cable in the right position when not in use. A deck hand would feel for the cable with a grappling hook, remove it from the water, and attach it to the winch at the prow of the boat. The *Whitehorse* would then pull herself up against the current until she could take over again under her own steam.

While the river pilots were highly skilled and experienced, some accidents did happen. On one occasion the *Whitehorse* broke a paddle-arm and we had to be assisted by the *Yukon Rose,* a much smaller vessel, which was lashed to the side of the *Whitehorse* to steady her against the downstream current. On another occasion a miscalculation brought leafy branches and tree limbs crashing into the upper deck when she veered too close to the bank too soon.

I left the *Whitehorse* at Carmacks on July 23, 1951, and returned to Whitehorse. But later on I returned to the river boats and was hired on as a deck hand for the tourist run from Whitehorse down to Lake Laberge and back.

The *Klondike II,* on which I also worked, was an almost exact replica of the *Klondike I* which had run aground in 1936. The original steamer was constructed by the British Yukon Navigation Company in 1929. With a superior design over other paddle-wheelers to that date, the *Klondike I* was able to carry 300 tons of freight without having to push a barge in front. The *Klondike II* was 210 feet long, 42 feet wide and nearly six feet deep. Launched in Whitehorse in 1937, she could carry 1,363 tons. Her boilers came from the old *Yukoner,* which had been left to rot in the Whitehorse shipyards, and the wreck of the *Klondike I.*

Although she was also used as a passenger ship, from 1937 to the early 1950s the *Klondike II* carried mainly cargo. Before the completion of the Whitehorse-Mayo road, one of her jobs was to pick up silver-lead concentrate at the mouth of the Stewart River, where it was brought down by the *Keno* and other smaller paddle-wheelers from the Mayo mines. By the 1950s, however, her days as a working cargo vessel were numbered and she was being used more and more as a passenger cruise ship only. By 1952 the *Klondike II* was making regular round trips between Whitehorse and Lake Laberge, with only an occasional freight run. By that time there was no more silver-lead concentrate from the Mayo mines to be delivered to Whitehorse.

Passengers boarded the steamer about noon for the down river run to Lower Laberge, where, according to Robert Service's famous poem, "The Cremation of Sam McGee," a miner from Tennessee was cremated in the boiler of the derelict stern-wheeler *Alice May.* During the evening the purser of the *Klondike II* did his best to get the passengers to sing songs

*The **Keno** docked at Stewart, Yukon. This steamer is now permanently beached at Dawson City.*

and evoke some of the atmosphere of the old gold rush days. The evening was rounded off with a public reading of Service's poems. We then returned to Whitehorse, where the passengers disembarked and continued their tours.

The *Klondike II* was completely refitted in 1954 as a tourist cruise ship at a cost of $100,000. Unfortunately, the tourist trade needed to keep her afloat did not develop until much later. By then it was both too late and, paradoxically, too early for the old steamer, for the later influx of tourists which might have saved her from becoming a museum piece did in fact take place.

Between June 15 and August 26 of 1955 the *Klondike II* made her final trips and was then permanently beached. Later she was moved to Whisky Flats, on the bank of the Yukon River at Whitehorse. Here, on Canada Day, July 1, 1981, the old steamer, newly decorated for the tourist trade, was opened to the public. The end of an era had been reached.

There is an epilogue to this story, in which I also played a part. It was the completion of a highway system linking Whitehorse with Mayo and Dawson City that finally put the paddle-wheelers out of commission. But it was the final link of what is now called the Klondike Highway, from Stewart Landing (now known as Stewart Crossing) to Dawson, that delivered the final deathblow.

The completion of the all-weather road from Whitehorse to Mayo about 1948 had already eliminated the need for paddle-wheelers on the Stewart River, because the silver concentrate from the Mayo District was then trucked by road to Whitehorse. A reconnaissance survey of the present Stewart Crossing-Dawson route was made in 1949, and in 1951 the final survey line was cut for the new road. After leaving the river boats, I worked on this survey party as an axeman and chairman under A.J.H. Litzenburger, then engineer for the Department of Resources and Development in the Yukon. Our job was to complete the final survey.

We drove from Whitehorse to Stewart Landing on the bank of the Stewart River to cut the survey line from there to Dawson City. The first few days were spent fighting forest fires which

had crossed the area where we were to begin work. Finally we were able to load our supplies on a barge pushed by one of the long narrow power-driven river boats often used by hunters and trappers on the Yukon River. The first part of our trip ran parallel to the Stewart River to a point beyond the McQuesten River near the site of the old roadhouse which serviced the winter trail from Whitehorse to Dawson.

The procedure was as follows: we set up a camp on the river-bank and then walked back several miles to begin cutting a line three feet wide to mark the course of the projected highway. When we had worked to a point several miles beyond our camp, we again loaded up the barge and moved our camp "leap-frog" fashion to a new site farther down river. We continued leapfrogging in this way until we reached the point where the Stewart River veers off in a southwesterly direction toward its conjunction with the Yukon River. Then we sent the boat and barge back to Stewart Landing and proceeded cross-country on foot toward Dawson City. The job began in summer, with us wading across the McQuesten River holding the survey chain over our heads to keep it out of the water, and ended well into the winter with us chopping holes in the ice of the Klondike River for drinking water.

Today a bridge replaces the old ferry at Stewart Landing and the tourist can drive in comfort along that portion of the highway parallel to the Stewart River down which we pushed our way 35 years ago. But the Klondike Highway also meant the end of the Yukon paddle-wheelers, and the last steamer was withdrawn from service about the time this final link was completed.

The Yukon River is now strangely silent. The paddle-wheelers are gone, although numerous visitors annually make the trip down river from Whitehorse to Dawson in private craft. But with the exception of Carmacks, where the Klondike Highway crosses the Yukon River, and a few families recently reported still living at Fort Selkirk and Stewart Island farther down river, the many river-bank communities which once serviced, or were serviced by, the steamboats, have long since been abandoned. It was far different in the summer of 1951.

It is with nostalgia tinged with regret that I now realize that, in a sense, I was instrumental in helping to bring the era of the paddle-wheelers to an end.

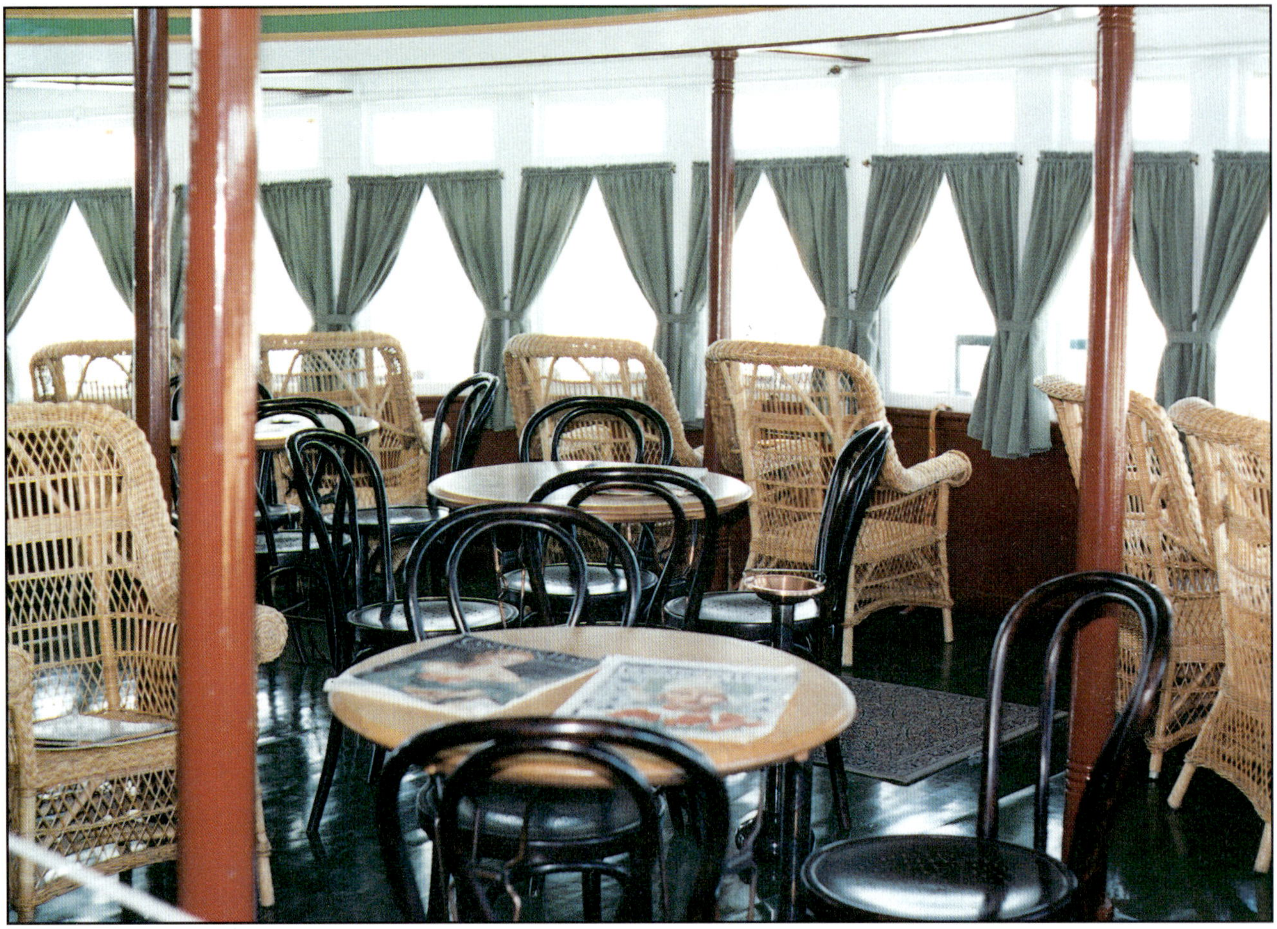

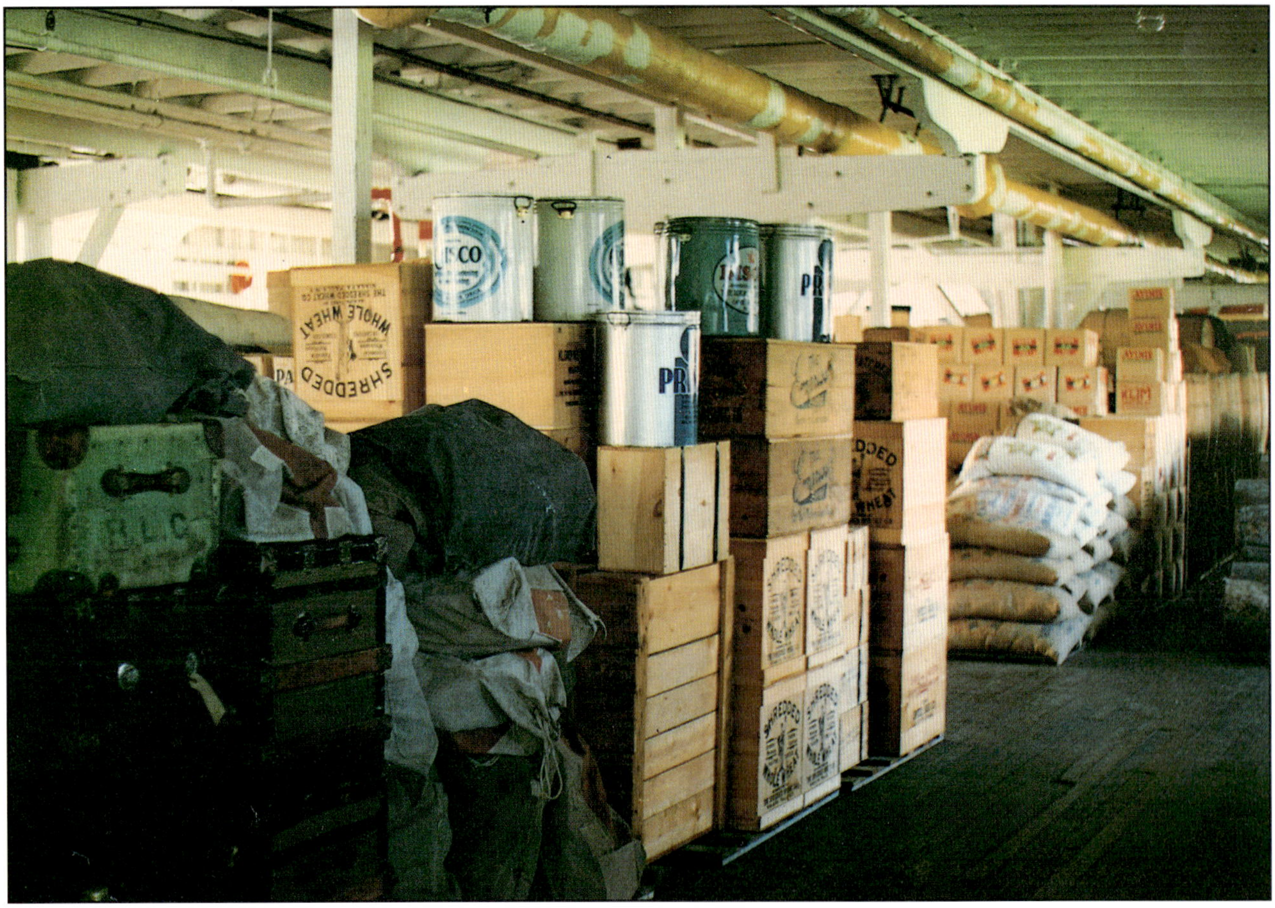
SHREDDED WHOLE WHEAT
KLIM

(Above) The wheelhouse of the Klondike *at Whitehorse.*
(Top right) The Casca *in winter drydock, January 1950.*
(Right) The old Yukoner *in winter of 1950.*
(Opposite page, top) The first class lounge on the Klondike *as it appeared in real life. In fact, some of the wicker chairs are originals, while the balance are exact reproductions.*
(Opposite page, bottom) A simulated load of typical freight on the Klondike.
(Bottom right) The steamship graveyard, a few miles downstream from Dawson.
(Below) Deck chairs outside the first class lounge on the Klondike *in 1988.*

JACK DALTON PIONEER TRAIL BUILDER

After an exciting career as a cowboy, gunfighter, logger, seaman, trader and miner, Dalton made his way to the Alaska-Yukon country in 1883. Following the discovery of gold in the Klondike, he established a toll road from Haines Mission to Fort Selkirk.

WHEN Jack Dalton pumped four bullets into Matt Egan on a winter day in 1883 in Burns, Oregon, a series of events was set in motion that would bring the adventurous young cowboy fame and fortune far to the north in Alaska and the Yukon.

On that December day in Burns, Jack's name was not Dalton; it was Miller. Born in 1855 in what would later be known as the Cherokee Strip of Oklahoma, Jack Miller learned the cowboy trade in Texas. Drifting from ranch to ranch through the southwest, he eventually worked his way north into the eastern Oregon cattle and timber country. There, in the spring of 1882, Jack found work as a buckaroo for the Devine and Todhunter outfit, where he stayed as a reliable hand for over a year.

In 1883 Miller left his ranch job and went into the mountains north of Burns to run a small logging operation. Lumber brought high prices at the ranches of the vast sage lands to the south, and those who were willing to endure the rigors of getting timber out of the mountains could make good money.

Among Jack's logging camp crew was a cook named Matt Egan. Two or three days before Christmas, Jack fired Egan and hired in his place a buxom, middle-aged widow. The irate Egan took off for Burns and began drinking heavily. The more he drank, the more he brooded.

A day or two after Christmas, Miller came to town for supplies. According to witnesses, he had not been there long when he was accosted by Egan, who loudly berated him for doing such a dirty trick. Miller, known for his quick temper and fighting ability, was cool and collected. Jack calmed his angry ex-employee by advising him to sleep it off and telling him that there was no reason they could not be friends. Temporarily appeased, Egan retreated for some further consideration at Broady Johnson's Saloon, and Jack Miller went about his business, gathering supplies.

According to the later recollections of Maurice Fitzgerald, who was in town that day, the truce between Egan and Miller was short lived. Egan, coming out of the saloon, saw Jack's horse tied to a post across the street. Soon Jack came out of Walsh Smeltser's saloon and started walking toward his horse. Egan called out to Jack and motioned for him to come over. Miller walked toward Egan briskly, his arms swinging loosely by his sides.

Egan stood motionless until Jack was close, then suddenly drew a pearl-handled Smith and Wesson revolver from under his coat. As he did so, Miller crouched and lunged at him. He grabbed Egan's wrist and forced it up as the gun went off, the bullet passing over Miller's shoulder.

Then, with his free hand, Miller pulled his own gun, a Colt Bulldog, and raised it to fire. But Egan caught Jack's gun hand just as he shot, forcing it down so that the bullet went into the ground at Egan's feet.

The two men stood for a few seconds, each holding the other's gun hand. The shots had gathered a crowd, but no one moved to interfere. Both men were strong, but Miller slowly forced Egan's gun upward and brought his own in line with Egan's body. He quickly sent four bullets into his opponent's stomach. Egan slumped to the ground and died.

Flushed with the excitement of near death and aware that several toughs, possibly friends of Egan, were standing in the crowd, Miller picked up the dead man's revolver and, armed now with two guns, strode to the saloon. No one in the group attempted to challenge Miller, and soon he quieted down, turned Egan's gun over to the hotel-man, and rode back to his logging camp.

The small community of Burns buzzed with news of Egan's death, and rumours were whispered of other shooting scrapes involving Jack Miller. Although the general opinion of witnesses was that Miller had been justified in shooting Egan, the law was not so sure.

For a few days after the Egan killing, Miller was left alone at his mountain camp. But soon more trouble headed his way, this time in the person of Sheriff Wallace Travillion of Baker County, to the north. Travillion had a warrant for the arrest of Miller on a charge of horse stealing in his district. Warned of the sheriff's presence in Burns by a friend, Miller considered it an appropriate time to seek his fortune elsewhere. Avoiding the town, he struck southwest over the sage plains to California.

Miller made his way to San Francisco, and in 1884 he shipped out for Alaskan waters on a sealing vessel. He had signed aboard under a new name, one that he would use for the rest of his life — Dalton.

Though the record of this period of his life is sparse, it is known that Dalton spent some time in the arctic that same year. The ship was seized by authorities for fur-seal poaching, and Dalton, along with the rest of the crew, spent a year in the territorial jail at Sitka.

Upon his release, Dalton stayed in Alaska, prospecting and exploring along the southeast Alaska panhandle at a time when few white men were in the country. In 1886 he signed on as a "cook and man of all work" with the *New York Times* expedition to the Yukon under Lieut. Frederick Schwatka.

Early in 1890, while he was in San Francisco after prospecting north of Juneau for several years, Dalton was approached by explorers Edward J. Glave and A.B. Schantz with an interesting proposition. *Frank Leslie's Illustrated Newspaper* of New York had engaged Glave and Schantz to make an exploration up the Chilkat River in southeast Alaska from the coast to the interior reaches of the Yukon. The passage would lead through the Saint Elias Mountains, the massive barrier range separating Alaska from Canada. Glave and Schantz wanted Dalton as a guide. Jack agreed, and in the spring began the adventure that would bring him wealth and fame.

The men knew that for hundreds of years Indians along the Chilkat River used three separate routes through the otherwise impassable Saint Elias Range. The hazardous Indian trails over the later famous Chilkoot and White passes were already known. But another trail, an easier but more mysterious way through the mountains, was said to exist farther up the coast. The Chilkat people guarded the route jealously, for it was the trail they used in a trade monopoly with the Indians of the interior.

On April 30 the six-man party, headed by E.H. Wells, landed at Pyramid Harbour, Alaska, near the present town of Haines. Five days later, after readying their canoes, they began their ascent of the Chilkat River en route to, they hoped, the Yukon. For the first two days, the men made slow progress up the Chilkat, spending much of their time pulling and pushing the canoes, wading in the water or floundering along the shore in the thick underbrush. On May 7 the small party reached the Chilkat Indian village of Klukwan. There they hired four additional Indians to assist in packing the equipment over the mountains. Leaving the canoes at Klukwan, they continued their journey on foot two days later.

They were now in unknown country. Leaving the Chilkat Valley after a few miles to follow a smaller river, the Klehini, they found that the forested, brush-filled, narrow river valley quickly gave way to a steeper climb at the foot of the Saint Elias Mountains. The men trudged along rocky slopes with towering Saint Elias peaks on all sides, glistening in their dazzling whiteness.

Dalton and Glave recorded that the old secret Indian trace ascended rapidly, winding around huge rocks and along rushing, glacier-fed streams. They slipped along the sides of glaciers and waded through snowbanks, dodging tangled underbrush in the gulches.

Finally, they reached the summit of Chilkat Pass and began a long, gradual descent through wide alpine valleys. Dalton noted the presence of grass in the valleys, abundant graze for stock. They were well into what was then called the Yukon District and on May 24, having located the way over the mountains, they began the return trek. They divided into two groups, Dalton and Glave returning by a roundabout course back to the coast, while Schantz and Wells followed another route.

The exploration had been a success; they had found and followed the mysterious Indian path to the interior. The forbidding Saint Elias Mountains had been breached.

Glave, seeing the potential of an interior trade route, decided to return with Dalton in the spring of 1891 to check the feasibility of taking pack horses over the mountains. In 1892, Glave wrote an article entitled "Pioneer Packhorses in Alaska" for *The Century Illustrated Monthly Magazine* in which he described the preparations:

"We equipped ourselves at Seattle with four short, chunky horses weighing about 900 pounds each, supplied ourselves with the requisite pack-saddles and harness, stores and am-

(Right) Some members of the North West Mounted Police and the "Mysterious 36" at one of the log barracks at Pleasant Camp in 1898.

(Opposite page, top) The NWMP detachment buildings at Dalton Post c1900.
(Opposite page, centre) The remains of what may have been an original "Dalton sled" at Dalton Post in 1988.
(Opposite page, bottom) An old hand-made saw at Dalton Post in 1988.

(Below) The remains of what appears to have been the main buildings at Dalton Post in 1988. The heavy gauge screen over the window openings was probably placed there by fishermen or campers as a precaution against grizzlies, which are numerous in the area.

A herd of cattle bound for Dawson along the embankment of the Dezadeash River at Champagne Landing, 1898.

munition, then embarked on board a coast steamer, and sailed north from Puget Sound, through the thousand miles of inland seas, to Alaska. We disembarked at Pyramid Harbour, which is by far the most convenient point, from which to start for the interior. No horses had ever been taken into the country, and old miners, traders, and prospectors openly pitied our ignorance in imagining the possibility of taking pack-animals over the coast-range. The Indians ridiculed the idea of such an experiment; they told us of the deep, swift streams flowing across our path, the rocky paths so steep that the Indian hunter could climb in safety only by creeping on his hands and knees."

When Dalton and Glave were not deterred by these disparaging reports, the Indians, whose monopoly would suffer greatly if the expedition proved successful, hinted that violence would be used to stop them. "However," wrote Glave, "when we were ready, we saddled up, buckled on our pistol-belts, and proceeded on our journey without any attempt at hinderance save by verbal demonstration."

The expedition, despite some setbacks and many difficulties, proved that it was possible to bring animals into the Yukon by way of the Chilkat Pass.

Glave left the Yukon shortly after and never returned. He went to Africa the following year, where he was killed in 1895. Dalton remained in the area, first at Juneau, and then at Haines Mission, where in 1894, he leased land for a trading post and a hotel. He also ran a small trading sloop that serviced the little southeast Alaska port settlements. Nothing further was done with the "trail" over Chilkat Pass; it was waiting for something big to happen in the interior. There had been a number of minor gold discoveries in the Yukon, and the feeling was shared by many that something was about to break open.

During this time Dalton killed another man. A drifter named Jack McGinnis was a loud bully who took pleasure in terrorizing fellow cannery workers at Chilkat. One day in March 1893, McGinnis was in the Chilkat saloon when someone asked about a sloop that had arrived in port. McGinnis knew all about it. He said the sloop belonged to a bootlegger and was bringing a load of whisky for the Indians. Bootlegging to the Indians was one of the lowest crimes in Alaska, as elsewhere, and nothing to spread loose talk about, particularly when it was not true. The sloop belonged to Dalton, not a bootlegger. He had worked hard to build his reputation for honest dealing with Indians as well as whites, and he was not about to have it sullied by a blowhard such as McGinnis.

Dalton heard what McGinnis had been saying and went looking for him. McGinnis was new to the Chilkat country and did not know Dalton. When Dalton approached him at the cannery, McGinnis was happy to repeat the story about the "bootlegger's sloop." Dalton called him a liar, said he was the owner, and demanded a retraction. McGinnis refused, trying to bluff his way out of the situation. Dalton's response was to draw his gun and shoot McGinnis six times. He then surrendered to the marshal. A trial was quickly convened and Dalton was acquitted. He was an honest trader, as everyone knew, and the consensus was that McGinnis got what he deserved.

In August 1896, George Carmack and his Indian brothers-in-law, Skookum Jim and Tagish Charlie, discovered gold nuggets in the gravel of Rabbit Creek, a small tributary of the Klondike River. Their discovery led to the richest gold strike in history. Word reached the outside world the following spring, and by late summer of 1897, the Klondike gold rush was on.

By this time Dalton was a seasoned businessman in the Chilkat area and he immediately set in motion plans to develop a toll trail to the goldfields. Though the routes over Chilkoot and White passes were shorter, they were much steeper and more tortuous than the old Chilkat trail. In July 1897, Dalton hired a professional surveyor to map and survey his new personal trail to the Klondike following the historic Chilkat route.

That summer Dalton and an old Indian crew brushed out the trail through the thickest underbrush, moved boulders,

(Above) A view of the Chilkat Cannery and surrounding settlement in 1899. It was here that Dalton killed Jack McGinnis.
(Below) A view of a three story frame building, spirit houses, etc., of the Klukwan Indian village, not far from Pyramid Harbour, Chilkat River, 1898.

and cleared dead trees. In the high country, over Chilkat Pass and beyond, they used dynamite to blow rock obstructions in the trail. Originally, Dalton had started his trail at Haines Mission. However, because of difficulties such as quicksand and rapids, by the spring of 1898 he had switched the starting point to Pyramid Harbour, some 20 miles away.

From Pyramid Harbour, the 350-mile-long trail followed the Chilkat and Klehini rivers northwest for 50 miles, then turned north to ascend Chilkat Pass. The trail passed through sweeping alpine tundra, dropping down into the rolling hills and plateaus of the Yukon interior. It then followed the Nordenskiold River to its mouth on the Yukon River. The distance from Pyramid Harbour to the Yukon River was 305 miles. The trail continued along the south side of the Yukon another 45 miles to Fort Selkirk. There the Dalton Trail ended, and river steamers and large rafts were used to float the remaining 200 miles down-river to Dawson.

By the spring of 1898, Dawson, in the heart of the Klondike goldfields, had grown from a smattering of tents to a boom-town of 30,000 people and at the time was the largest city west of Chicago and north of San Francisco. There were an estimated 60,000 people in the Klondike looking for gold.

Dalton was finding his gold another way. His trail was the only way to get animals to the Klondike. Stock could not be brought in over the Chilkoot Pass, with its 30 degree grades and final climb of 1,200 icy steps to the summit. The White

(Top left) A member of the NWMP in dress uniform posing in doorway of log barracks either at Dalton Post or Pleasant Camp, June 1898.

(Top right) The remains of another log building at Dalton Post today.

(Above) Salmon traps in the Klukshu River at the edge of Klukshu Indian village in July 1988. The village itself was deserted.

(Right) Four members of the "Mysterious 36" and an Indian pose for a photograph in front of a tent at Champagne in 1898. Most of the men are carrying revolvers.

(Opposite page) The remains of the Dalton Trail, which was later improved by the government, as it approaches Yukon Crossing. Although heavily overgrown, the trail is still clearly visible. (Left inset) The remains of what was originally a stable at Yukon Crossing. (Right inset) Interior of cabin at Yukon Crossing with bushes growing in the middle of the floor. Note the low doorway, which forced all who entered to stoop.

Some men sitting around an open tent on the Dalton Trail. It was here that a fee of $2.50 per horse and $2 for every head of cattle was collected for travelling the Dalton Trail.

Pass route was worse. It was an endless bog even in winter, and good time on it was one mile per day. Leading through crevice-like canyons almost totally impassable for pack-horses, it became known as the "Dead Horse Trail."

Dalton placed log cabin roadhouses and tent camps along his trail, and he obtained permission form the U.S. government to charge a toll. The Canadian border was 55 miles up the trail from tidewater, and though he received clearance from the Dominion of Canada to build the trail, he could not collect tolls in Canada; therefore they were collected on the American side. The fee for cattle, horses and mules was $2.50 each; for sheep, 50¢. Foot travellers paid $1 each, unless they were Indians, in which case they passed free.

Dalton was not the first entrepreneur who tried to impose a toll on his road, but he was the first to make it stick. In Pierre Burton's *Klondike,* he describes one party that decided to drive a herd of beef cattle over the trail without payment. "As they were about to set out, Dalton appeared with rifle and six-gun and told the leaders he would shoot the first man or beast who set foot on it. Then, as the party floundered through the bushes and scrub brush alongside the trail, Dalton kept guard in splendid isolation on the right of way for 300 miles to show he meant business."

In his 1892 article "Pioneer Packhorses in Alaska," Glave described Dalton as ". . .a most desirable partner, having excellent judgement, cool and deliberate in time of danger, and possessed of great tact in dealing with the Indians. He thoroughly understood horses, was as good as any Indian in a cottonwood dugout or skin canoe, and as a camp cook I never met his equal."

Glave's opinion, it would seem, was not one shared by many in the Yukon. Dalton was a tough man to tangle with and not very well liked. In addition to the two killings already de-

scribed, Dalton once beat a man severely for trying to establish a saloon on his property. During the summer of 1898, he was in trouble again, this time with Indians.

When Dalton moved his trail from Haines Mission to Pyramid Harbour, it was no longer necessary to ford or ferry across the Chilkat River. Unfortunately, the Indians had been charging tolls for ferrying goods across the river, and Dalton's actions had dried up that income. One Indian in particular, Hard Working Jim, took exception to this and took a shot at Dalton. The situation became tense and Captain Yeatman and some soldiers had to be sent over from Dyea to maintain order.

Fortunately, Hard Working Jim surrendered peacefully and the soldiers were able to return to Dyea, only to be called right back because of another disturbance. Dalton's employees had taken over the historic Indian route and were charging both Indians and whites for its use.

While the majority of gold seekers on foot made use of the shorter Chilkoot Trail, many others, particularly those with horses, went by way of the Dalton Trail. The largest traffic over the trail consisted of livestock. It was well suited for horses, cattle, and sheep and played an important role in supplying booming Dawson with meat and pack animals. Grass along the trail was plentiful, and even with the high crossing of Chilkat Pass the trip to Dawson could be made in two months.

The summer of 1898 was a dream come true for former Texas and Oregon cowboy Jack Dalton. The hoards of miners in Dawson wanted beef — lots of beef — and Dalton provided it. By August of that year he had made himself a hero to the hungry Klondikers by bringing in over 2,000 head of cattle. The stock was shipped up from the States to Pyramid Harbour. There Dalton organized the drive, collected the tolls, and drove the cattle over his trail to Fort Selkirk, where they were

Jack Dalton, fifth from left without hat, poses for photograph with five men of the group "The Mysterious 36" outside a log cabin on June 9, 1898.

slaughtered and rafted down to Dawson. Dalton shrewdly purchased 80 of them on the hoof at Pyramid Harbour, and sold them at Dawson for $750 each, for a total of $60,000, a fortune in those days. During that magic summer he also brought in 2,000 horses, and hundreds of sheep, selling them in Dawson at a handsome profit.

Later that year Dalton formed a partnership with several eastern Oregon ranchers and brought up 1,000 head of cattle in one drive. They sold in the Klondike for $300 per head, or $300,000, a major share going to Dalton.

Other cattlemen and sheepherders used the Dalton Trail too. Charles Goodall drove 300 sheep over the Chilkat Pass, mindful of the ever-present, unpredictable Alaska brown bears, and cattlemen Simpson and Lewis drove 250 steers to the Yukon River in September 1898.

Dalton's trail provided him with other business opportunities as well. He started the Dalton Pony Express Company, providing riding and packhorses for those who did not want to walk the 350 miles or chance the perilous Chilkoot or White passes. For this service he charged $250. Many of the women, including "soiled doves," who went to the Klondike did so astride a Dalton horse.

Dalton also freighted in supplies on his packhorses and specialty built "Dalton sleds." For a time, he had a contract to carry mail and Klondike news dispatches from Dawson out to the Pacific Coast Steamship Company's mail ships at Pyramid Harbour.

He maintained three trading posts and roadhouses along the trail. One called Dalton Cache was located on the Canadian border at a place known as Pleasant Camp. The second was 50 miles farther up the trail at Dalton Post, and he kept a station that he called Champagne at about the halfway point on the trail. The log structures of the three trading posts still

stand and can be seen via the Alaska Highway and the Haines Highway.

The Dalton Trail received most of its use during the summers of 1898 and 1899. By July 1900, the White Pass and Yukon Railway had been completed and was carrying passengers and freight from Skagway to the Yukon, lessening the importance of the Dalton Trail. By 1902 the colourful but hectic days of the gold rush were over. The easy pickings were gone, and new strikes at Nome and Fairbanks had lured the prospectors and miners to other golden dreams.

Dalton abandoned his trail and closed the trading posts in 1906. The Dalton Trail was unique in the Alaska-Klondike gold rush in that it was the only trail built largely by one man and successfully operated as a toll road.

Dalton, who had profited greatly from the Klondike madness, invested in a hotel at Haines, a large cannery at in Pyramid Harbour, and several gold mines. In 1913, ever in search of adventure, he prospected for coal in the Chickaloon district of Alaska and brought out the first shipments from that rich area. He also helped locate and survey the Alaska and Copper River railroads, and for some years he owned a line of stern-wheelers plying the waters of southeast Alaska.

In 1919 Dalton sold most of his Alaska interests and moved to Yakima, Washington, where he bought a ranch and fruit orchard. In 1921 a group of Yakima businessmen interested the old adventurer in sailing to British Guiana to check on their holdings in the diamond diggings there. He returned to Washington the next year, but in 1923 was off again to British Guiana, this time to hunt gold.

In 1943 Dalton was living on the Oregon coast, and on December 16, 1944, he passed away in San Francisco at 89 years of age. Jack Dalton had come a long way from that winter day in Burns, Oregon, and his gunfight with Matt Egan.

INDEX